MW00439442

Lake Erie Journal

Guide to the Official Lake Erie Circle Tour

Ohio, Michigan, Pennsylvania, New York, Ontario

Lake Erie Journal

Guide to the Official Lake Erie Circle Tour

Ohio, Michigan, Pennsylvania, New York, Ontario

By Scott Carpenter

BIG RIVER PRESS

Acknowledgments

The author wishes to thank the many communities, chambers of commerce, visitors bureaus and other travel and tourism agencies whose cooperation made this book possible. Special thanks to the Great Lakes Commission, Ottawa County (Ohio) Visitors Bureau, Fred Snyder of Ohio Sea Grant, the New York State Seaway Trail, Mark Hicks, Sparky Bowman, and Art Weber

CREDITS

Photographs: By Scott Carpenter unless otherwise credited.
Maps: Mark Hicks
Design: Mark Hicks

New York Seaway Trail logos and War of 1812 used with permission of Seaway Trail, Inc.

Copyright © 2001 by Scott Carpenter

All rights reserved. With the exception of brief quotations in critical reviews or articles, no part of this work may be reproduced or transmitted in any form or by any means, electronic or mechanical, including photocopying, recording, or any information storage and retrieval system, without permission in writing by the publisher.

Published by Big River Press, P.O. Box 130, Millfield, OH 45761

Printed in the United States of America.

ISBN 0-9643309-4-6

In Loving Memory of Lois H. Kline
April 25, 1918 - June 14, 1992

Preface

The major efforts by the United States and Canada to return Lake Erie to a healthy, viable lake took place roughly between the time I entered kindergarten and my high school graduation — a lifetime then, but in hindsight only a blip.

As teens, my friend Chris Schwind and I were oblivious to these historic changes when we dared each other to defy the nor'easter-driven waves crashing over the pier at Metzger Marsh not far from our suburban Toledo homes. Somehow we made it to the light pole at the end and back without being swept over the side, more amused by the tremendous force of nature than afraid.

Most of my encounters with the lake in those days ostensibly had something to do with fishing. I waited patiently from boulders strewn along the shore for a catfish to take my smelly bait, endured the chop of a grouchy lake aboard small boats in search of perch, and waded waist-deep into the muddy Maumee River for white bass and walleye. In truth, most outings had more to do with fun than fish and the outcomes were usually in keeping with my priorities. But each trip was an adventure.

Later, as a newspaper columnist, I set out on a more serious trek to write about the significance of the lake to the region that surrounds it and to demonstrate the important role this magnificent body of water played in the lives of millions of people in two countries.

From a small island in Put-in-Bay Harbor where college students go to study Lake Erie first hand, I learned about the state of the lake, its ever-changing makeup and its colorful, even checkered past. I talked with scientists and activists, charterboat captains and commercial fishermen, park rangers and plant managers — anyone who had a stake in the lake. I found both agreement and controversy about issues dealing with public policy, competing uses and common courtesy, but I also noted a shared sense of ownership in the region's greatest natural attribute. And it was still an adventure.

Having traveled the Erie shore many times, camping on islands, feeling the spray of Niagara Falls, wading creeks with my daughters Rachel and Lauren, and sharing sunsets on secluded beaches with my wife, Beth, I feel a sense of ownership too.

Looking back, it was inevitable that I would write a book about Lake Erie and my friend Chris would become an avid boater and member of the U.S. Coast Guard Auxiliary. The seeds planted 20 years ago on the piers and rocky shores of the western basin have grown into a lifetime obsession for both of us.

Scott Carpenter
Toledo, Ohio
2001

CONTENTS

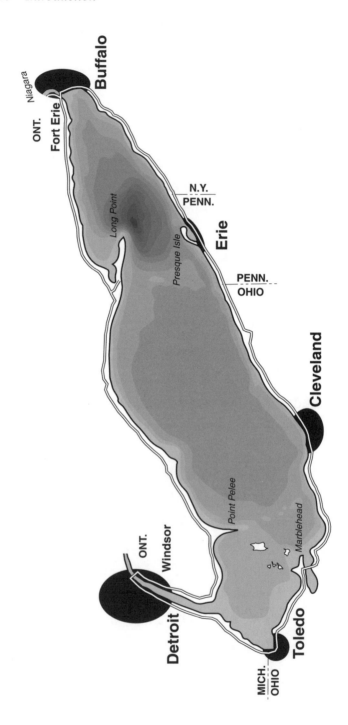

Introduction

Around A Great Lake

From a country highway in southern Ontario, Erie is a thin blue ribbon bordering vast fields of red tomatoes. In Ohio and New York, it is the backdrop for sprawling cityscapes of skyscrapers, smokestacks and arenas. Sunbathers bask on beaches built by a glacier in Erie, Pennsylvania, and rare plants and animals take refuge in a man-made marsh in Monroe, Michigan.

The scene out your passenger side window changes by the hour as you trace the shore clockwise around Lake Erie, the way this book is organized.

Some of the most popular tourist attractions in four states and a Canadian province are found on Lake Erie, from historic sites to charming vineyards, elegant resorts to tacky tourist traps. The region has islands, parks, zoos, museums, casinos, amusement parks and outlet malls; some of the best birding and fishing on the continent, and Niagara, the world's most famous waterfall.

The Lake Erie Circle Tour is a nearly 700-mile driving route completed in 1990 by the Great Lakes Commission as part of the Great Lakes Circle Tour, a 6,500-mile scenic route through eight states and two Canadian Provinces.

*Various signs designate the
Lake Erie Circle Tour through
Ohio, Michigan, Pennsylvania,
New York and Ontario.*

Green and white signs mark the Circle Tour route in Ohio, Michigan and Pennsylvania, while blue and white signs identify the tour along the north shore in Ontario. In New York, the tour overlaps part of the larger New York Seaway Trail, a National Scenic Byway that continues to the Atlantic coast.

Along the way, side trips, sometimes marked by brown signs, lead the way to local attractions such as a lighthouse, a historic downtown district, or maybe a century-old covered bridge.

In New York, significant sites from the War of 1812 create a museum without walls. In Ohio and Pennsylvania, monuments pay tribute to war hero Commodore Perry. On the other side of the lake, Fort Malden and Fort Erie tell the other side of the story.

Elsewhere on the tour are ghosts of another era, the mid-1800s, when fleeing slaves sought shelter on their secret journey on the Underground Railroad.

In other places, vineyards dominate the shore. Award-winning wines are part of the bounty of a rich soil and a moderate climate in a region that also produces everything from apples to zucchini.

If this were a race, you could easily encircle Lake Erie in a matter of hours. As a vacation, you could occupy yourself for a week. Make it a mission to explore the shore, savor each outing and return often, and you may never have another boring weekend.

Lake of Change

Mentioning plans to spend a family vacation on the shores of Lake Erie 25 or 30 years ago would have provoked blank stares or worse, belly laughs. Your choice, if not your sanity, would have been called into question. A lot has changed in three decades since a fire on the Cuyahoga River ignited a generation of change.

It was 1969. If the fish in Lake Erie didn't suffocate they were so contaminated with mercury they were not fit to eat. Birds like the double-crested cormorant hatched with crossed bills and other fatal deformities caused by pesticides. Mayflies didn't hatch at all.

Today it's a toss-up whether to declare Lake Erie the walleye or smallmouth bass capital of the world. The water is clear, the beaches are busy and nobody's laughing at Erie anymore.

Mark Hicks Photo

Lake Erie's walleye and smallmouth bass fishing are unequalled. Perry's Monument on South Bass Island looms in the background

Lake Erie is part of the largest fresh surface water system in the world — a 94,000 square-mile bluish blotch on the planet called the Great Lakes. These five "Freshwater Seas" — Superior, Michigan, Huron, Erie and Ontario — contain 6 quadrillion gallons of water, one-fifth of the world's fresh surface water and 95 percent of the U.S. supply. Their coastlines stretch 10,900 miles along the borders of eight states and two Canadian provinces.

Along these shores are North America's industrial and agricultural heartland, a multi-billion dollar outdoor recreation and tourism industry, a world-class maritime transportation system and an incomparable fishery.

Lake Erie, named for the Iroquois word for cat, is the fourth largest of the Great Lakes by area, but smaller than Ontario in volume. It is the eleventh largest lake in the world, but 25 times smaller than Superior. Call it the little Great Lake.

As the shallowest and most southerly of the lakes, Erie is the warmest and most biologically productive, supporting the largest freshwater commercial fishery in the world. The lake's shallow, saucer shape also makes it especially vulnerable to fluctuating water levels and wind setups that can push water from one end of the basin to the other, sloshing it back and forth like a bathtub. Erie reacts quickly to these fluctuations, piling up waves and sending them crashing down on the shore. The lake can be unpredictable and dangerous, like its namesake, the cat.

Erie's shallow depth also contributes to its environmental vulnerability and a propensity for rapid change. Its small volume intensifies water quality problems because it has less ability to dilute pollution than the larger lakes, yet its short retention time allows it to cleanse itself of these impurities more quickly than the other lakes. While water that flows or precipitates into Lake Superior stays in the lake for about 180 years, Erie holds its water for just three years.

Legislation and international cooperation in the 1970s led to improvements to municipal sewage treatment plants, a ban on phosphorus in laundry detergents and increased use of no-till and reduced-till farming practices to keep the soil from washing into streams. Because of these measures, the amount of phosphorus going into the Great Lakes decreased by more than half from 1968 to 1982.

Perhaps one of the best illustrations of Lake Erie's comeback was the mid-1990s return of the mayflies. The odd-looking

Mark Hicks Photo

One of the best indications of Lake Erie's improved water quality is the return of mayflies.

little worms with wings have become so thick again in some parts of the lake that the dead insects have to be shoveled from sidewalks and plowed from roads the morning after a hatch.

While it is too soon to declare a full recovery — leaking landfills, contaminated sediment, invading exotic species and urban sprawl are vexing problems we have only begun to contend with — Erie's condition is headed in the right direction. More importantly, the way the lake is viewed by society has changed since the "dirty water" days. People have rediscovered the lake, reinvested in it, and expect more from it. We have learned all too well how quickly it can change.

Lake Erie Facts

Ninety-five percent of Lake Erie's water comes down the Detroit River from the upper lakes via the St. Clair River, Lake St. Clair, and from numerous smaller tributaries. The remainder comes from precipitation in its own watershed. Erie empties into Lake Ontario through the Niagara River and the man-made Welland Canal.

Here are some other Lake Erie facts:

Length...241 miles
Breadth...57 miles
Average Depth...62 feet
Maximum Depth...210 feet (off Long Point, Ontario)
Volume...1,116 cubic miles
Water Surface Area...9,906 square miles (more than 5 million acres)
Drainage Basin Area...22,720 square miles
Shoreline Length (including islands)...871 miles
Elevation...571 feet
Water Retention/Replacement Time...2.6 years
(shortest of the Great Lakes)

(Sources: Environment Canada; Ohio Sea Grant; Michigan Sea Grant.)

CIRCLE TOUR: Blue and white signs mark the Lake Erie North Shore Route, as the Circle Tour is called north of the border. From the Ambassador Bridge, the tour follows Huron Church Road to Highway 20 south and east along the Detroit River and Lake Erie shore. In Leamington, the route follows County Road 34 (formerly Route 3). The name (or number) changes at each county border, but the Circle Tour follows the same road (old Route 3) all the way to the US border.

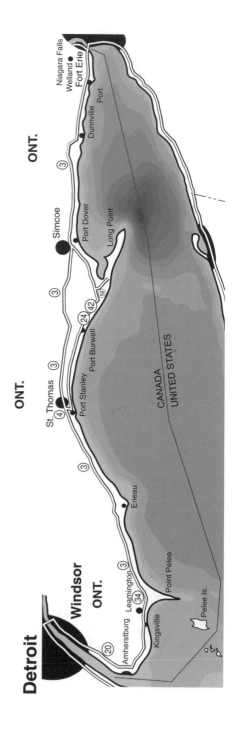

Section 1

The North Shore

AMBASSADOR. The name beams in red letters from towers above 27,000-tons of steel spanning the Detroit River, linking the United States and Canada. Up to ten million vehicles a year traverse the one and three-quarter mile deck suspended 152 feet above the river that both divides two nations and connects each with the world. The Ambassador Bridge is the gateway to the industrial and agricultural heartland of two countries, the crossroads of the continent — the pinnacle of a circle around Lake Erie.

At its opening in 1929, financier Joseph A. Bower called the privately owned bridge a "visible expression of friendship." Today, the Ambassador is the busiest border crossing in North America and the conduit for more than one-quarter of the estimated $1 billion a day in trade between the largest trading partners in the world. In fact, traffic is increasing at such a rate that a second bridge has been discussed. Given the economic and social significance of the Ambassador, perhaps the new river crossing should be named "Prosperity."

The cities of Windsor and Detroit on either side of the bridge are amiable ambassadors of their respective nations facing each

Windsor Convention & Visitors Bureau

The Ambassador Bridge spans the Detroit River, linking the United States and Canada.

other over a narrow border, forming what amounts to a binational metropolis. And while they can hardly be called twin cities (Detroit is nearly five times Windsor's size), there is a family resemblance. The cities were settled around the same time, although Detroit was nearly 200 years old by the time Windsor was officially incorporated in 1896. Both share French roots still evident today in the streets named for their heroes. Both are known as the Motor City and each count the "big three" automakers among their largest employers. More recently, both have turned to gambling as a means of injecting new money into their sagging "Rust Belt" economies. At the same time, Windsor and Detroit maintain their own distinct identities.

Similar, yet different, describes the two cities as well as the nations they represent. Subtle, charming differences give visiting Americans the flavor of being in another country, if not exactly culture shock. North of the border, the native tongue pronounces "about" more like "aboot," bacon tastes suspiciously like ham, country clubs offer curling as well as golf, and doughnut shops propagate like burger joints in the states. The money looks funny, cigarettes come in odd-shaped boxes and speed limits seem extraordinarily high (although speed demons will be quite disappointed when kilometers are converted to miles per hour). Crossing the border is not much different than exiting a toll road interchange where a nosy attendant in a small booth asks you where you're going and when you plan to return.

There are few places in the world where people can step cross the border with such ease. Nowhere is the congenial coexistence of two nations as evident as here, where the Lake Erie Circle Tour crosses the aptly named Ambassador Bridge.

Notes on Entering Canada

Besides the Ambassador Bridge, there are two other options for entering Windsor-Essex County from the United States: The Windsor-Detroit Tunnel, a mile-long passage 75 feet under the Detroit River, is the only international underwater car tunnel in the world. Built in 1930, a year after the Ambassador, it is the fastest way to cross from downtown Detroit to downtown Windsor. The slowest, but most enjoyable way to cross the border is by ferry from Sandusky, Ohio, to Kingsville or Leamington, Ontario, via Pelee Island.

When crossing the border, a guard may ask you to state your citizenship, destination, the purpose of your visit and how long you expect to stay in Canada. That said, you're usually on your way in a matter of seconds. There are times, however, that the crossing can be a hassle. You may need to show your vehicle registration or personal identification. On rare occasions, you may even be asked to pull over so someone can search your car.

U.S. citizens entering Canada may need proof of U.S. citizen-ship for each occupant of their vehicle. Passports are unnecessary, but a birth certificate along with a photo I.D. such as a driver's license may be requested. Naturalization papers or U.S. Alien Registration Card (better known as a Green Card) is required of those for whom such documents apply.

Americans driving in Canada need a Canadian Non-Resident Interprovince Motor Vehicle Liability Insurance Identification Card, a long way of saying proof of insurance. Simply ask your automotive insurance agent for a "Canada card."

A traveler in any foreign country will want to familiarize himself with such things as currency exchange rates and customs allow-ances, both of which are subject to change. Visitors to Ontario can claim a refund for some of the seven per cent Goods and Services Tax (GST) paid on accommodations. They may also qualify for a refund of the eight-percent RTS (Retail Sales Tax) on goods purchased in Canada for use outside the country. There are limits on the amount of goods, including alcohol and tobacco, allowed in and out of Canada, some of which depend upon the length of stay. For information, stop in the Duty Free Shop near the Ambassador Bridge.

Note also the differences in U.S. and Canadian laws. For example, handguns are strictly prohibited in Canada. The legal age to enter gambling establishments or to drink or purchase alcoholic beverages is 19. Seatbelts are required and radar detectors are prohibited. You can buy Cuban cigars in Canada but you can't bring them home to the U.S.

Not only are road signs posted in both English and French, motorists should pay attention to the metric speed limits. A kilometer equals 0.62 miles, so 80 kilometers per hour is about 50 miles per hour; 100 kph is 62 mph, etc. Temperature is measured in degrees Celsius. To figure the approximate temperature in Fahrenheit, double the Celsius number and add 30. For example, 10 degrees Celsius equals approximately 50 degrees Fahrenheit.

Windsor Convention & Visitors Bureau

Windsor on the Detroit River.

Chapter 1

Windsor

W indsor is a lively place with a vibrant downtown full of shopping options, restaurants and night spots, a broad riverfront view of the Detroit skyline and enough greenspaces to classify the City of Roses as a garden spot. Its main streets hum with activity day and night as more than eight million visitors a year flood this city of 200,000. But the number of people who come here to shop, dine and smell the roses pales in comparison to the number who come to roll the dice.

The tenth largest city in Canada changed almost overnight in 1994 when gambling came to town. Windsor was transformed into Canada's little Las Vegas with a single casino that quickly became one of the top tourist destination in the nation — and that was even before the permanent casino opened its doors.

The first Casino Windsor outgrew its temporary quarters so quickly that a riverboat casino was added to handle the overflow. These stopgap gambling parlors where more than 20,000 visitors spent a minimum of $1 million each day closed in 1998 when the real gaming palace opened to even larger crowds in its permanent home on Riverside Drive East.

Windsor Convention & Visitors Bureau

Casino Windsor in its permanent home on Riverside Drive East.

Today, the two million square-foot Casino Windsor complex sprawls over six city blocks in the riverfront section of downtown called City Centre. Owned by the Ontario government and operated by the gambling giant ITT Caesars World and Hilton Hotels, the complex has 100,000 square feet of gaming space on two levels and an attached 23-story hotel tower with 389 rooms.

Inside, past the 60-foot waterfall, gamblers find 135 table games and nearly 3,000 slot machines ranging from 25 cents to $100. The complex never closes and has enough amenities that gamblers never have to leave, including a health spa and cigar shop, restaurants, live entertainment, a video poker bar, a bar called Canadian Club (after one of the city's prominent businesses) and a skywalk connecting with a 3,000 car parking garage.

The casino's impact on Ontario has been tremendous. Tourism in Windsor increased 250 percent from 1995 to 1998, pumping hundreds of millions of new dollars into the local economy. Nearly eight million gamblers spent $750 million at the temporary casinos in 1997 alone. That's American dollars — 80 percent of Casino Windsor's patrons are from the U.S. side of the border.

Beyond the glamour and glitz of the casino, City Centre, the district that includes Ouellette Avenue and Pelissier Street, also has more than 300 shops and services including open-air sidewalk

Windsor Convention & Visitors Bureau

Blackjack is one of many games of chance you may enjoy within the two million square-foot Casino Windsor complex.

cafes, boutiques and theaters. Dieppe Gardens at the foot of Ouellette Avenue and nearby Ambassador Park offer panoramic views of Detroit's sparkling skyline dominated by Renaissance Center, and the ocean-going ships and "lakers" that pass beneath the bridge. What makes the view truly unique is that this is the only place in Canada where you look north to the United States.

Windsor's rich ethnic diversity shines in its downtown where the fashions and flavors range from French to Polish, Ethiopian to Vietnamese, Jamaican to Chinese. The ethnic heritage of the city is most apparent in its cultural districts.

Via Italia, the strip along Erie Street, is a Little Italy with imported foods, clothes and gifts and a large number of the city's many pizzerias (it has more pizza shops per capita than any other town in Canada).

Via Italia, the strip along Erie Street, is a Little Italy with imported foods, clothes, gifts and a large number of the city's many pizzerias.

Ottawa Street Village Mall has more than 45 stores with a distinctive Eastern European flavor. More than a dozen restaurants serve up dishes from Indian to Polish. The Ukrainian National Federation and the Hungarian Society are both headquartered here.

This ethnic diversity is celebrated each year during the first two weekends in June with the Carrousel of Nations festival featuring 30 or more "villages" with different cultural or ethnic themes set up at various locations around town. Windsor and Detroit jointly celebrate the International Freedom Festival for two weeks each year around July 1.

Entertainment in Windsor runs the gamut from male and female strip clubs notorious for their bachelor and bachelorette parties to a comedy club and dinner theater. Cultural arts also thrive with a symphony and a dramatic arts school at the University of Windsor. Entertainment venues include The Chrysler Theatre at the Clearly International Center, the Capitol Theatre & Arts Center and Villanova Festival Theatre.

Parks & Shoreline

At its core, Windsor is a working class, industrial town known for making automobiles and whiskey. On the surface, it presents a

Dieppe Gardens is located at the foot of Ouellette Avenue. Nearby Ambassador Park offers panoramic views of Detroit's skyline, and the ocean-going ships and "lakers" that pass beneath the Ambassador Bridge.

Windsor Convention & Visitors Bureau

Windsor Convention & Visitors Bureau

Coventry Gardens, two miles east of downtown on the Detroit River, overlooks Detroit's Belle Isle. The centerpiece of the park is the Peace Fountain.

more refined image. The City of Roses earns its nickname by maintaining a variety of natural and cultivated greenspaces.

Dieppe Gardens and Ambassador Park are part of a chain of parks and gardens that stretches for nine miles along the Detroit River from the bridge to the city's eastern border. The community credits the foresight of its forefathers for setting the waterfront aside. Such prudent planning is rare on Lake Erie, where many communities seem to have only recently discovered their waterfronts. Dieppe Gardens is also the launch point for the *Aurora Borealis*, which offers daily lunch, brunch, dinner and sightseeing cruises. A monument to Canadian and U.S. veterans of the Vietnam War is located at Assumption Park, another scenic spot on the river.

Coventry Gardens, two miles east of downtown on the Detroit River, overlooks Detroit's Belle Isle. The centerpiece of the park is the Peace Fountain, a computer-controlled water show that sprays patterns 70 feet in the air. The fountain is lighted at dusk.

Ojibway Park, on Matchette Road at Broadway, is in the center of a 315-acre natural area made up of tallgrass prairie, pine-oak forest and savanna. A nature center and self-guided tours give visitors a chance to learn more about these habitats which contain more than 700 types of plants, including at least 100 considered rare.

The Queen Elizabeth Sunken Gardens and Lancaster Memorial Rose Garden in Jackson Park at Ouellette Avenue and Tecumseh Road together feature 12,000 rose bushes made up of 450 varieties of roses. The adjacent veterans memorial has more gardens centered around a World War II bomber.

There are also 25 miles of beaches in Windsor and surrounding Essex County, which is bordered on three sides by Lake Erie, Lake St. Clair and the Detroit River.

Add to the series of greenspaces the linear parks created by a network of bicycle paths, including a converted rails-to-trails greenway.

Historic Sites

◆ The Fransois Baby House is the oldest brick building on the riverfront and was used by General William Hull and his Kentucky Militiamen when they crossed the river in 1812 in a disastrous bid to take Ft. Malden. The Hiram Walker Foundation restored the building, which today houses the Windsor Community Museum, made up of a variety of exhibits related to the community's heritage, including a children's hands-on history room.

◆ Mackenzie Hall Cultural Community Centre, the former Essex County Courthouse built in 1855, is the centerpiece of Olde Sandwich Towne, the oldest English Settlement west of Montreal.

Willstead Manor, built between 1904 and 1906, is a 36-room Tudor-Jacobean style English manor house.

Windsor Convention & Visitors Bureau

Windsor Convention & Visitors Bureau

Hiram Walker and Sons Limited, distillers of Canadian Club whiskey since 1852, offers free one-hour tours to visitors.

◆ The Historic Essex Railway Station on Station Street in Essex was once part of the Canadian Southern Railway Line. The fieldstone building has been restored to its former glory and now houses a retail art gallery and historical center.

◆ The Serbian Heritage Museum exhibits traditional arts and crafts, paintings and drawings related to Windsor's Serbian culture.

◆ Willstead Manor, built between 1904 and 1906, is a 36-room Tudor-Jacobean style English manor house. Operated by the Windsor Department of Parks and Recreation, the house is decorated for the holidays in December and hosts an outdoor craft exhibit in the spring. In late summer, it is the site of a classic car show.

Windsor-Area Attractions

◆ The Devonshire Mall is a modern shopping center with 150 stores. One of the attractions of the mall is The Art Gallery of Windsor, with 2,500 works of art related to Canadian culture.

◆ Windsor City Market has more than 70 permanent vendors selling an abundance of fresh-from-the-farm produce, poultry, eggs, dairy products, flowers and meats.

◆ The home of Hiram Walker and Sons Limited, distillers of Canadian Club whiskey since 1852, is a popular tourist destination. Free one-hour tours allow visitors to see how whiskey is made in the waterfront distillery, located next to the Via Rail Station on Riverside Drive. The surrounding Walkerville neighborhood was a separate community before joining Windsor in 1935.

The North American Black Historical Museum in Amherstburg houses cultural artifacts and artwork, including a permanent exhibit about the Underground Railroad.

◆ There are other gaming options besides Casino Windsor. Windsor Raceway on Highway 20 south of town offers harness racing with indoor viewing and live and intertrack wagering. It is open year round. About a dozen bingo emporiums in and around the city offer gambling seven days a week, year round.

◆ Suchiu Galleries in Essex is an art and framing center devoted to the works of internationally known artist Ronald Suchiu.

Following the North Star

An estimated 40,000 slaves followed the North Star across the border to make new homes as free people in Canadian towns like Sandwich and Amherstburg. These refugees joined hundreds of former slaves brought to Lake Erie's north shore by British Loyalists after the U.S. Revolution and set free by an 1833 declaration by King William IV of Britain. After the Civil War, half the refugees returned to live in the United States.

Today, half a dozen significant sites in African-American history are preserved in southwestern Ontario. The Windsor, Essex County & Pelee Island Convention and Visitors Bureau has a brochure with a map to each of the sites on the African American Heritage Tour.

Uncle Tom's Cabin Historic Site is a small farm in Dresden in northern Essex County where Josiah Henson lived out his 94 years after leading his family and 100 other slaves across the border from Sandusky, Ohio.

The John Freeman Walls Historic Site, near the town of Maidstone, also in the northern part of the county, is a log cabin built in 1846 by a fugitive slave from North Carolina whose story is told in the book "The Road that Led to Somewhere," by Dr. Bryan Walls. The site is host to the International Freedom Festival and Gospel Festival each June.

Refugee slaves built the Sandwich Baptist Church, Windsor's first black church, in 1821. It is preserved in the Olde Sandwich Towne section of Windsor.

Learn more about these and other sites at the North American Black Historical Museum in Amherstburg, which houses cultural artifacts and artwork, including a permanent exhibit about the Underground Railroad.

Windsor Convention & Visitors Bureau

The War of 1812 capped 60 years of conflict that began with the French and Indian War in the 1750s. This re-enactment takes place at Ft. Malden National Historic Site.

Amherstburg and the War of 1812

Legend has it the man who fired the first canon ball over the Detroit River in 1812 killed his best friend. Unlikely perhaps, but symbolic of a war often depicted as disorganized, half-hearted, even senseless.

The War of 1812 is memorable for the burning of the White House by the British, the bloody battle of New Orleans and the patriotism-inspiring scenes of "bombs bursting in air" described by a lawyer named Francis Scott Key in his poem "The Star-Spangled Banner." Less memorable are the battles waged in western Lake Erie in the early days of the war, a time America might prefer to forget.

The war capped 60 years of conflict that began with the French and Indian War in the 1750s, continued through the American Revolution and for another 30 years of skirmishes with the Indians of the western frontier.

The reasons for the war were complex and far removed from most citizens of either country, and unpopular on both sides of the border. In its zealous opposition of Napoleon in Europe, the British blocked the importation of goods, virtually shutting down American foreign trade. In the process, they seized American cargo ships, sometimes pressing their crews into service for the Crown. The audacity of the Royal Navy infuriated the War Hawks in Congress. By the time England finally loosened most of its restrictions on American trade in the spring of 1812, it did not know that the United States had already declared war.

Even before the naval blockades began, America was angry with the British for offering arms and support to the Indians who inhabited land in Canada and Florida — land that Americans were eager to settle during the late 1700s and early 1800s craze for expansion. Worst of all, British politicians and businessmen supported attempts by the great Indian war chief Tecumseh to form a league of Indian tribes to fend off the land grab.

At the time, the States had nearly 8 million citizens compared to 500,000 in British North America. Upper Canada was not only outnumbered, but many of the settlers were estranged Americans

***Built in 1796 as Fort Amherstburg on the Detroit
River, Fort Malden was the base for combined
British and Indian forces during the War of 1812.***

who had moved there for the cheap taxes. Surely, the Americans
thought, taking Canada would be like taking candy from a baby —
"a mere matter of marching," as one war lord put it.

Emboldened by the odds so heavily in their favor and angered
by a British and Indian sneak attack on Fort Mackinaw a month
earlier, the Americans brazenly marched over the border to take
Fort Malden at Amherstburg in 1812. Nobody would have pre-
dicted they would fail, let alone that they would lose Detroit in the
process. America was stunned. After all, they had sent William
Hull, a hero of the revolution, backed by the intrepid troops of the
Kentucky militia. Not once did they consider the possibility that it
would be Isaac Brock, a young Canadian general, who would
emerge from the battle a national hero.

Hull, it seems, was no longer the man remembered for his
strategic prowess and valor. In one of the war's biggest blunders,
he had sent a small ship on ahead from his camp on the Maumee

River in Ohio carrying his luggage, which unfortunately contained his battle plans. It's a safe bet that Brock could not believe his luck when his troops captured the ship and learned details of Hull's campaign. He also read in letters written by Hull of the Americans' fear of Tecumseh and his Indian warriors, a fact he used to his advantage by spreading rumors that the Indians were out of control and bloodthirsty.

When Hull and his troops arrived in Detroit, Brock was waiting with a cannon assault. Fearing what might become of the occupants of Detroit — including his own family — at the hands of the Indians, Hull surrendered within a few hours without firing a shot. Accusations of treason and cowardice were directed at Hull, who was court-martialed. If not for his heroic service in the Revolution, he probably would have been hanged. Instead, he lived out his life in disgrace.

Fort Malden National Historic Site

You can almost feel the ghosts of the British soldiers on the neatly groomed grounds of Fort Malden National Historic Site. Built in 1796 as Fort Amherstburg on the Detroit River, the fort was the base for combined British and Indian forces during the War of 1812. The British destroyed the original fort when they were forced to retreat from the Detroit River frontier in September, 1813. The Americans who then occupied the territory began to rebuild it, but the work ended along with the war a few months later. The British used Fort Malden again as a key defensive post 25 years later to fend off attacks by rebels and American sympathizers during the Upper Canada Rebellion of 1837.

Today, the national historic site preserves the original earthworks, a restored barracks and an interpretive center. Historic re-enactors greet visitors, answer questions and fire off an obligatory shot from a musket. Fort Malden is located in the town of Amherstburg, 18 miles south of Windsor on Route. 20.

Nearby Navy Yard Park, where frigates were built to do battle in the War of 1812, is a scenic spot to linger by the river and watch the boats and freighters go by. From the park you see Boblo Island,

*The ubiquitous Canada goose runs a close second
to the maple leaf as Canada's most visible icon.*

once a thriving amusement park that, following a succession of
owners, went bankrupt and is now being carved up for homes and
condos. You can get there via car ferry from Amherstburg.

Where the Geese Go

The ubiquitous Canada goose, the large waterfowl easily
recognized by the white patch on either side of its black head, runs
a close second to the maple leaf as Canada's most visible icon. A
pair of conservation areas are famous among birders as places to
observe Canada's most prominent bird and the thousands of other
waterfowl, raptors and warblers that stop each spring and fall to
rest during their long migration.

The dean of Canada geese, not just in Ontario but in North
America, was a Kingsville man named Jack Miner. In the early
1900s, Miner spent many days pondering why the pond on his
farm near Kingsville was not loaded with the birds. Where did they
go? Acting on his curiosity, Miner bought 13 domesticated Canada
geese and turned them loose on the pond as live decoys to see if
their wild brethren would join them. Year by year, slowly at first,

The Jack Miner Sanctuary welcomes wildlife watchers. A nature center overlooks the pond and provides interpretive information.

the geese did return — 11 in the spring of 1908, 32 the next year, about 400 the year after. By 1911, thousands of birds were stopping regularly at Jack Miner's place.

That curiosity satisfied, Miner turned his pondering to the bigger question of where the geese came from and where they went. To answer these questions, he attached bands to the birds' legs inscribed with his address (usually accompanied by a Bible verse). For the next 30 years, Miner collected data from his experiment, charting each location where one of his birds was spotted. Strangers would notify him because of the instructions on the leg bands. Miner's charts were the first to track the migration route of the giant birds from South America to the Hudson Bay. Modern-day researchers still use the banding technique to continue the work he began. At Miner's farm, about 100,000 geese and as many ducks have been fitted with tags since 1909 — each still containing a short verse of scripture.

Miner's work attracted such well-known fans as Henry Ford and baseball legend Ty Cobb, who brought attention and money to the Bird Man's homespun research center. Miner became so revered that he has been dubbed the Father of Conservation, and the week of his birthday, April 10, is known in Canada as National Wildlife Week.

The Jack Miner Sanctuary, operated by a private foundation, still welcomes wildlife watchers who come in spring and fall to witness the spectacle of thousands of migrating geese covering the fields or soaring in V formation overhead. A Nature Center over-looks the pond and provides interpretive information. As Miner wished, the sanctuary is closed on Sunday and there is no gift shop.

Located on the Lake Erie Shore on County Road 50 between Amherstburg and Harrow, Holiday Beach is another haven for geese, although waterfowl are not the birds for which this famous resting stop is best known. Holiday Beach is one on of the continent's premier locations for viewing the fall migration of hawks, eagles and other raptors funneling in to the mouth of the Detroit River. More than 75,000 birds of prey are counted here on average each year, including 40,000 broad-winged hawks and 11,000 turkey vultures.

Birders also flock to the conservation area to watch the spring and fall migration of birds big and small from the walking trails or the three-story observation deck overlooking the marsh. On a single day in late September, observers have recorded up to 200 hummingbirds and as many as 50,000 bluejays flying overhead. Like the raptors, songbirds gather in the area before or after making the trip around Lake Erie on their biannual journey. Other migrants include dragonflies, bats and Monarch butterflies.

Holiday Beach also offers family camping, a trout pond, waterfowl hunting and a sandy beach. The facility is run by the Essex Region Conservation Authority, which operates 13 conservation areas.

Sunbathers enjoy a day on the Lake Erie shore at Kingsville, Ontario.

Amherstburg to Leamington

Kingsville is Canada's southernmost town, a pleasant place with maple tree-lined streets, quaint shops and restaurants and sandy beaches. Ferries arrive and depart from the docks headed for Pelee Island and Sandusky on the Ohio shore.

◆ Park House Museum, adjacent to Fort Malden, is the oldest house in the area and contains a small community museum and decorations from the 1850s. It also features heritage craft demonstrations, from candle dipping to tinsmithing.

◆ Colasanti's Tropical Gardens in Ruthven (between Kingsville and Leamington) is a showplace of tropical plants and flowers, cactus gardens and exotic birds in 20 connecting greenhouses on 32 acres. Part trade market, part theme park, Calasanti's also has a petting zoo, kids rides, miniature golf, an apple orchard, crafts and wicker for sale and a cafe. It is a popular tour bus destination.

◆ County Road 50 leads to Colchester, a scenic town with a modern harbor where a charter boat service offers sightseeing tours to the many shipwrecks around Point Pelee. Also on Route 50 is the John R. Park Homestead & Conservation Area, a working 1850s farmstead with a blacksmith shop and sawmill operated by the Essex Region Conservation Authority.

◆ Agricultural research is the business of the Harrow Research Center in the town of the same name. Tours of the experimental fields are offered free of charge.

Wine Trail

As the most southerly point in Canada, Essex County enjoys the most moderate climate and the longest growing season in the country. This is also Canada's wine region. Pelee Island Winery in Kingsville, Colio Wines and LeBlance Estate Winery in Harrow and the D'Angelo Estate Winery near Amherstburg all offer tours. Five wineries in all make up the Essex County Wine Trial, which is marked by road signs and detailed in a brochure from the Visitors Bureau.

More Information

Casino Windsor
377 Riverside Drive East
Windsor, ON N9A 7H7
800-991-7777
www.casinowindsor.com

Essex Region Conservation Authority
360 Fairview Ave West
Essex, ON N8M 1Y6
519-776-5209
www.erca.org

Jack Miner Bird Sanctuary
P.O. Box 39
Kingsville, ON N9Y 2E8
www.jackminer.com

North American Black Historical Museum
277 King St.
Amherstburg ON N9V 2C7
519-736-5433

Windsor, Essex County & Pelee Island
Convention and Visitors Bureau
Suite 103
333 Riverside Drive West
Windsor, ON N9A 5K4
800-265-3633
www.city.windsor.on.ca/cvb

Windsor & District Chamber of Commerce
2575 Ouellette Pl.
Windsor, ON N8X 1L9
519-966-3696
www.windsorchamber.org

CIRCLE TOUR: In Leamington, the North Shore Route follows the Talbot Trail, marked as Highway 3. Along the way, there is an option to detour from the marked route and instead follow the county roads that hug the shoreline. Either way, all roads west lead to Fort Erie on the Niagara River.

Chapter 2

Along the Lakeshore

Most Americans cross the Ambassador Bridge, head straight for Highway 401 and race off to Niagara Falls or Toronto, sacrificing the pleasures of a country drive for a little speed and a couple of extra lanes. Thanks to these hasty travelers, the scenic route is less crowded for the rest of us. Farm markets dot pastoral roads in Canada's South. Vineyards stretch to the water's edge, tobacco hangs in drying shacks in the fields, and miles of unspoiled beaches, marshes, swamps and woods await tourists in the many parks and preserves along the lakeshore.

There are no bustling cities, football stadiums or casinos to distract from the scenic resort communities sprinkled among farm towns, fishing villages and nature preserves where you will find some of the most picturesque settings on all of Lake Erie. Come to the north shore for the quiet, the parks and the scenery, and consider the small towns you happen upon along the way a pleasant surprise.

Leamington is such a place, and you don't need a map to find it. Just follow the red splotches on the road made by tomatoes fallen from trucks bound for the H.J. Heinz Company plant. You

The Leamington tourist information booth, shaped like a tomato, is a tourist attraction in itself.

will know you have arrived when you see the Big Tomato, as it is simply known, a 16-foot-tall tourist information booth that has been a community icon for more than 30 years.

At the main intersection, trucks and tractors pulling trailers loaded with the fruit of area fields come from all directions destined for the processing plant, Leamington's largest industry and a major part of the town since 1908. A Tomato Festival, naturally, is held in late August.

The tomato may be king here in Canada's "sun parlor," but it has plenty of company. Essex County, which stretches from the Detroit River to Point Pelee, is blessed with a mild climate that ensures the longest growing season in Eastern Canada and some of the most diverse crops in the country. Roadside produce stands offer a cornucopia of fresh-from-the-field asparagus, eggplant, peas, potatoes and fruit, from gooseberries to grapes, peaches, plumbs, pears, nectarines and strawberries. You might want to pick up some popcorn for the campfire and maple syrup for the morning pancakes. A brochure by the Windsor, Essex County & Pelee Island Convention and Visitors Bureau lists farm tours, produce markets and related attractions.

Leamington, the gateway to Point Pelee National Park, is also known for its bumper crop of birds. Banners across the main drag and signs in store windows and on lampposts welcome back the birders who come to the region to witness the spring and fall

Serious birders make up a large part of the Leamington area's tourists.

migrations of more than 300 species of songbirds, hawks and waterfowl. In the birding world, Pelee is considered one of the premier sites on the continent.

Pelee Island

The fruit of a different vine covers the countryside of Pelee Island, home to a 265-acre vineyard owned by the Pelee Island Winery. The winery is in Kingsville on the mainland, but a wine pavilion and a retail store are located on the island, which lies along the same latitude as the wine-producing regions of northern California and Europe, making it attractive to vinticulture for more than a century.

Sitting on the porch of a Victorian bed and breakfast, a glass of Pinot Noir in hand, savoring the solitude and lulled by a gentle breeze off the lake, it's difficult to imagine that a famous battle took place here. It was March 3, 1838 when infantry, militia and First Nations soldiers crossed the ice and routed 300 American supporters of the Mackenzie rebellion from the island.

Today, tourists descend upon Pelee, the largest of all the Lake Erie Islands. The 10,000 acre island, nine miles long and three and one-half miles wide, has a small business district with restaurants and shops, cottages, beaches, a campground and marina. A local pheasant farm hosts an annual hunt in October.

The Pelee Island Heritage Centre, open daily from May to

mid-November, explains the island's unique natural and human history with exhibits ranging from rare plants to historic artifacts and shipwrecks.

There are two provincial parks on the island. Lighthouse Point, located on a northeastern spit, is a 237-acre nature preserve that is home to several rare species including the blue racer and Lake Erie watersnake. At the tip of the spit are the remains of an 1834 lighthouse. There are no park facilities. Fish Point, on a southwest spit of the island, is an important stopover for migrating birds. There is a small parking lot but no other comforts. For real solitude, venture by boat to East Sister Island, a remote provincial park with a natural beach.

Middle Island, a nature preserve south of Pelee near the U.S.-Canada border, is the most southerly point in Canada.

Getting There

Pelee Island is a one and one-half hour ferry ride from Kingsville or Leamington aboard the MV Pelee Islander or the MV Jiimaan, which both offer car ferry service. Ferries run from March through December, depending on lake and ice conditions. The same ferries operate between Sandusky, Ohio, and Pelee Island, a one-hour, forty-five minute trip.

Point Pelee National Park

"The Flies are Biting Today," reads the handmade sign taped to the toll booth window. A dozen people sitting in a tram waiting for a ride to The Tip at Point Pelee National Park swat the pesky insects from their necks and ankles. Relief comes instantly — finally — as the tram driver starts the truck and mercifully pulls the sightseers into the cool breeze of a mid September afternoon.

The trip is quick, 5 minutes or so. You could walk or bike, but you can only drive there in winter when the fragile ground is frozen. However you reach The Tip — flies or no — you are rewarded with a panoramic view of Lake Erie and the satisfaction of reaching the most southerly point of mainland Canada.

A canoe is the best way to explore the marsh at Point Pelee National Park.

The name Pelee, French for "bald," describes the barren point, one of the most recognizable geographic features on Lake Erie. Point Pelee and another prominent protrusion, Cedar Point on the Ohio shore, mark the beginning of the western basin, the shallowest, warmest and most biologically productive part of the lake.

Point Pelee, one of the smallest of Canada's 38 national parks, is a delicate oasis. Just eight square miles in size, it has a complex of habitats unequalled in parks many times its size. Pelee is part of a narrow band of vast deciduous forest rarely found in Canada. Known as the Carolinian Zone, the forest accounts for just one-quarter of one percent of the Canadian landscape. This environment exists this far north because of the moderating effects of the lakes that nearly surround southwestern Ontario.

The diversity of plant and animal life in the Carolinian Zone endows this region with more rare species than any other in

The boardwalk at Point Pelee National Park takes visitors out into the marsh.

Canada. Seven hundred and thirty types of plants, including 70 tree species, have been documented here, and there are at least 50 species of spiders and insects not found anywhere else in the country.

Diversity is the keyword for Pelee, which is made up of marshes, forests, fields and beaches. The marshes — what Indians called "the between land" because it is neither land nor water — are among the largest remaining in southern Ontario and are of international significance. Another kind of wetland found here is a swamp forest, distinguished from a marsh because of the dominance of trees. The star attraction of the open fields is the seemingly out of place prickly pear cactus, a protected species. Bordering Pelee's patchwork of habitats are 12 miles of golden sand, a harsh, constantly changing environment where only the hardiest plants survive.

Pelee is world renowned as one of the top birding spots in North America. At least 360 different birds have been recorded here. It is also known for its autumn waves of migrating Monarch butterflies, the highly recognizable orange and black insects that feed on the milkweed that grows here. The short-lived creatures fascinate nature lovers by their ability to migrate to distant South America, a trip that may require several generations to complete.

The challenge at Pelee is to manage this significant place for the benefit of both the native flora and fauna and the half-million people a year who come to enjoy it. For this reason, Pelee is a mostly wild place, with some strict rules to help keep it that way. Ongoing preservation and restoration projects are reintroducing the southern flying squirrel and fostering the growth of the bald eagle population.

That said, this is by no means a hands-off park. Day users enjoy a visitor center with interpretive displays, a small restaurant and a well-stocked nature-oriented bookstore. There are trails from 0.4 to 4 km long including an intriguing 1.4 km boardwalk into a marsh with two observation towers. Another trail leads to a partially restored 1840s homestead. Five beaches and six picnic areas are heavily used at peak times of the year. Campfires are permitted in designated areas, but no overnight camping is allowed.

Programs throughout the year cater to all ages, from workshops to guided canoe trips, films and lectures. A Friends of Point Pelee organization sponsors an annual Festival of the Birds, a Canada Day celebration, a butterfly count, fall and winter festivals, a Halloween hike and campfire, and a Christmas bird count.

Between The Tip and Pelee Island, visible in the distance, is Pelee Passage, an area of swirling waters said to have claimed at least 250 ships. The entire area is identified as an underwater preserve and a tourist trade has developed for diving on these wrecks, especially in recent years with Lake Erie's dramatic improvement in water clarity. Dive shops in Leamington and Colchester offer cruises for non-divers aboard boats equipped with underwater cameras to view the wreckage below. Dive charters take beginner and experienced SCUBA divers below for a hands-on tour of the wreckage. Some of the doomed ships rest in as little as 40 feet of water.

Area Attractions

Heading east from Point Pelee, the Circle Tour route cuts across the heart of the Canadian South, a region whose main crops

Hillman Marsh Conservation Area is one of the top spots in the region for viewing marsh wildlife.

are tourists and tomatoes. Farming and fishing communities mingle with summer resorts, wildlife areas and provincial parks.

◆ Hillman Marsh Conservation Area is one of the top spots in the region for viewing marsh wildlife. There is a visitors center and walking trail.

◆ Wheatley, the freshwater fishing capital of the continent, is home to Wheatley Provincial Park, a quiet base to camp while taking in the surrounding sites. The lakefront park, open April through mid-October, has four campgrounds with 210 sites. Natural features include shagbark hickory trees, spring wildflowers, migrating songbirds and butterflies, and three creeks for canoeing.

◆ North Buxton, a side trip off Route 3 north on Kent County Road 6, was originally a haven for fugitive slaves. It is one of the few remaining black Canadian settlements in existence, dating back to the pre-Civil War days. A museum memorializes this rich heritage.

◆ The resort towns of Erie Beach and Erieau are the region's playgrounds, known for excellent bass, pike, perch and salmon fishing. Erieau is the site of the annual Salmon Hunt held in July. It has a modern marina and sandy beach.

◆ Family-owned London Winery on Highway 3 west of Blenheim offers tram tours of the vineyard in summer.

◆ Rondeau Provincial Park, south of Morpeth, is made up of lush Carolinian forests, beach-maple forests, marshes, dunes and long, parallel beach ridges interspersed with valley-like depressions called sloughs. At least 334 bird species have been identified here, including bald eagles, which are sometimes spotted from the Marsh Trail. Rondeau also has 334 camp sites. The park is open year round.

◆ Ridgetown, which bills itself as "the friendliest town in Ontario," is a short side trip north. Victorian architecture, accommodations, museums, a game farm and an 18-hole golf course are among the reasons to visit.

◆ Back on Highway 3, Clearview Park has a campground and children's play area. The Greenview Aviaries Park and Zoo, open May through October, houses hundreds of tropical birds, waterfowl and other domestic and exotic animals on its 20 landscaped acres.

◆ Port Glasgow is a boater's and fisherman's dream, with private fishing charters, several marinas and launching facilities, and a fishery that includes salmon and pickerel.

◆ John E. Pearce Provincial Park, just south of Wallacetown on Highway 3, is a day-use park ideal for a picnic or a leisurely walk along the bluffs overlooking the lake.

St. Thomas and the Talbot Route

Talbot is a name seen often along Route 3. For much of the route, the road itself is called the Talbot Trail. Along the way is the town of Talbotville, just east of St. Thomas. Both are named for Colonel Thomas Talbot, an Irishman born in 1771 who first came to Upper Canada as a British officer at age 21.

After finishing his commission in England, Talbot returned to Canada with a land grant of several thousand acres from the British government. From his base at Fort Talbot on Lake Erie he began to build the Talbot Settlement with St. Thomas as its capital. The landlord ensured the development of his settlement by retaining rights to all property he sold until certain conditions were met by the buyer, namely that the land was cleared and a home was built. His vast landholdings encompassed 29 townships covering a huge portion of present-day southwestern Ontario and had a population of more than 30,000.

Talbot was a colorful character who wore a sheepskin coat and fox-fur cap with the ears and tail still attached and earned the title

Colonel in the local militia. He was a recluse who lived mostly in isolation in his Port Talbot "castle." The name of his capital city, St. Thomas, might be considered ironic because in his time Talbot was considered something less than a saint.

The land baron had no family and upon his death bequeathed the vast empire he had assembled over 50 years to a trusted personal servant. Talbot is buried in a courtyard at St. Peter's Anglican Church just east of the lakeshore hamlet of Fort Talbot.

Talbot Road began in 1890 to link the Talbot Settlement with other settlements east and west. Following the route of an old Indian trail, the corduroy road extended west along the north shore of Lake Erie to the Niagara River at Fort Erie and east to the Detroit River at Sandwich (now Windsor). Present-day Highway 3 follows much of the original Talbot Road.

Today, the town of St. Thomas, known as "The Flower City," is the center of this region with a population of around 30,000. It is the traveler's best bet on this stretch of the Lake Erie shore to find a place to spend the night. Victorian architecture and scenic parks, shops, restaurants and hotels make this community a pleasant stopover.

Area Attractions

◆ Yes, that is a life-size statue of an elephant on a hill in St. Thomas. The statue is a memorial to Jumbo, star of the Barnum & Bailey Circus. The animal was struck and killed by a train near here in 1885 and the monument was unveiled on the 100th anniversary of the prominent pachyderm's untimely demise.

◆ Aylmer, east of St. Thomas, has a restored 1874 town hall and opera house, a museum and a popular flea market. In March, birders gather at the Aylmer Wildlife Management Area to witness the annual return of 60,000 swans during spring migration.

◆ Tillsonburg is a modern community with shopping malls, boutiques and restaurants.

◆ Southwold Earthworks near Tillsonburg are what remain of a double-walled Neutral Indian fort.

◆ There are more hotels in nearby New Sarum on Route 3. For a taste of Canadian history, visit the Elgin County Pioneer

Museum located in an 1849 pioneer physician's home on Talbot Street.

◆ Highway 3 is "Tobacco Road." In Delhi, the tobacco capital of southern Ontario, a Tobacco Museum documents the history and technology of tobacco production from Indian times to present. The museum also has a restored sawmill. Along the way, notice the tobacco farms with their odd-shaped barns, or kilns, where the crops are hung to dry.

Lakeshore Detour

SIDE TRIP: At St. Thomas, you may opt to leave Highway 3 to follow the scenic shoreline. Go south on Highway 4 to Port Stanley and follow county roads 24 and 42 east to Long Point. There will be another option to get to Long Point from Tillsonburg.

At one time, Port Stanley was perhaps the premier tourist attraction on all of Lake Erie. Its beautiful beaches were the backdrop for a casino and a famous night spot called the Stork Club where in the 1830s people came by ferry from as far away as Buffalo to hear the big band sounds of entertainers like Guy Lombardo. Port Stanley today is still a popular summer resort. The bands and casino are gone, but its historic streets with boutiques, restaurants and an art gallery are inviting. The sandy beach is still considered one of the nicest on the north shore.

A commercial fishing boat is a common sight on the Ontario shore.

The Port Stanley Terminal Rail offers a scenic excursion on a passenger train between Port Stanley and St. Thomas. The seven mile trip crosses two bridges, parallels boat-lined Kettle Creek and stops at two historic rail stations. Volunteers restored this seven-mile stretch of the former London & Port Stanley Railway to give visitors a taste of life in the 1850s, when millions of people rode these rails to spend a weekend on the lakeshore.

Area Attractions

◆ Hawk Cliff, a bluff high above the lake, is touted as one of the best places in North America to witness the fall migration of hawks. Up to 20,000 hawks a day have been seen here in early September.

◆ Port Bruce Provincial Park is a small day-use park in the lakeshore town of the same name.

◆ Sparta, a short side trip off County Road 26 north on County Road 36, was settled in the early 1800s by Pennsylvania Quakers. Its unique architecture and shops makes it a worthwhile diversion.

◆ The oldest wooden lighthouse in Canada, built in 1840, is located on the harbor in Port Burwell. Port Burwell Provincial Park, adjacent to the harbor, has a swimming beach and summer activities such as evening campfires.

◆ Sand Hill Park has a 450-foot-tall pile of sand that has been growing and shifting for centuries. The Alton family has owned the private park since 1850 and today operates it as a campground and recreation area.

◆ The town of Vienna, just north of Port Burwell on Highway 19, is known for being the summer home of Thomas Edison and his family. Today it is home to Canada's first Edison museum.

Long Point

SIDE TRIP: From the lakeshore route, Long Point is located east of Port Burwell on County Road 42. From Tillsonburg, Long Point is a side trip south on Highway 59.

A sand dune at Long Point Provincial Park.

A warm wind sweeps the beach, sculpting sand into smooth, golden mounds garnished with green sedges, grass and trees. Most of Lake Erie's coast looks very different today than it did 100 years ago, but here on the north shore in the eastern basin a piece of the past survives more or less unscathed.

Long Point is the longest sand spit on the Great Lakes and one of Canada's most important and delicate natural areas. Part wildlife preserve, part provincial park, part private paradise, this sliver of land jutting 20 miles into the lake's deep end is recognized globally as an example of a natural Great Lakes coastal ecosystem. It also happens to be one of the prettiest places on the Lake Erie shore.

It took 4,000 years of wind and waves to create what we see today — a unique complex of habitats that includes long, uninterrupted beaches bordered by dunes and grassy ridges; wet meadows, woodlands and ponds. An inner bay fringed by marshes is an internationally important staging area for migrating waterfowl, especially the diving ducks that feed on wild celery and other aquatic vegetation that grows there.

The scenic shore of Long Point.

Because of its natural attributes, the peninsula and inner bay was designated in 1986 by the United Nations Educational, Scientific and Cultural Organization (UNESCO) as a World Biosphere Reserve. The designation places Long Point in a league of natural areas with such places as the nearby Niagara Escarpment and the far away Galapagos Islands, Serengeti National Park, the Florida Everglades and the Great Smoky Mountains.

A dozen decades before UNESCO discovered Long Point, a dozen businessmen of uncommon foresight recognized the point's importance and took steps to ensure its survival. The Long Point Company, a private sportsman club, purchased the Point from the Crown in 1866 and for more than a century maintained the natural resources that almost certainly would have been squandered out of greed, ignorance or indifference.

For the first half of the 1800s, Long Point was an unsavory place known for illegal prize fights, gambling and piracy. By mid-century, the natural resources were threatened as migrating water-fowl and other birds were being slaughtered by the thousands and uncontrolled, mostly illegal lumbering was destroying the protective cover, exposing large areas of the unstable point to erosion from wind and waves.

The Long Point Company put a stop to the poaching and plundering with strict rules for the property's use. Then in 1979, the group ensured the Point's continued protection by giving a large portion of the land to the Canadian people to be preserved as a national wildlife area.

Today, most of the peninsula remains closed to all but the wildlife that abound in this sanctuary in the heart of industrial Ontario. The Long Point National Wildlife Area extends for the last nine miles of the peninsula, stretching to the tip where a lighthouse still signals danger to passing ships. The Long Point Company retained about nine-miles in the peninsula's midsection, where it continues to operate one of the most prestigious hunting clubs in the world.

A small piece of the Long Point Peninsula at the end of the cottage-lined Highway 59 causeway has been set-aside for the public to enjoy. Long Point Provincial Park, south of the small farming and resort town of Port Rowan, is an outdoorsman's dream. The park has 261 campsites, some with hookups for water and electricity (or "hydro," as power is called in these parts). Campsites and picnic areas are within a short walk of the public beach. A small marina and boat launch provide access to the wide, shallow Inner Bay and its marshes, teaming with smallmouth and largemouth bass, northern pike, pickerel, salmon, trout and yellow perch. There is an adjacent public hunting marsh, but most of the marshes along the inner bay are privately owned, as is the Long Point Beach cottage community along the causeway.

Turkey Point Provincial Park, on the opposite side of the inner bay, is a larger park with 195 campsites on a bluff overlooking three miles of sandy beaches. Turkey Point offers more amenities than Long Point, including a golf course, marina, picnic sites, play areas, trails and programs led by the park staff. There are restaurants located nearby in the town of Turkey Point.

About halfway between Long Point and another sand spit, Presque Isle, on the south shore in Pennsylvania, Lake Erie reaches its deepest point, about 210 feet.

Ontario's Vacationland

Long Point is part of the Haldimand-Norfolk Region, Ontario's "Vacationland." The region has 4,000 campsites, 3,300 marina slips, 23 hotels, a dozen golf courses, cottage rentals, bed and breakfast inns, museums, historic sites, and annual festivals. More importantly, it has 110 miles of Lake Erie shore. The region's natural beauty and visitor-friendly towns offer a wide variety of distractions for travelers passing through or those looking for a base from which to explore Ontario's "deep south."

◆ On the Inner Bay between Long Point and Turkey Point is the town of Port Rowan, a pleasant place to stroll the streets or docks, peruse the shops or settle in for a fish dinner. The town holds an annual Tomato Festival on Labor Day weekend.

◆ The Backus Heritage Conservation Area in Port Rowan is a historic village with more than a dozen restored or reconstructed buildings including the oldest continuously operating grist mill in the province. One of 30 conservation areas owned and operated by the Long Point Region Conservation Authority, Backus offers visitors a glimpse at the peninsula's past through guided tours, special events and educational programs. Family camping, nature hikes, fishing and canoeing make the conservation area a vacation within a vacation while visiting the Long Point area.

◆ Simcoe, a town of 15,000, on Highway 3, is the largest community and the commercial center of the Haldimand-Norfolk

Boat garages at a marina in Port Rowan.

region. Simcoe lights up for Christmas. The annual Panorama of Lights celebrates the season with more than 60 lighted scenes made up of 50,000 bulbs depicting religious, ethnic and fairytale themes.

◆ The Brook Conservation Area, a Long Point Regional Conservation Authority site located in Simcoe, has walking trails including the Lynn Valley Trail, a former railroad corridor stretching 8 kilometers from Simcoe to Port Dover. The area also has scenic picnic and fishing spots.

◆ The Lynnwood Arts Centre in Simcoe is a public gallery located in an 1851 Classical Greek revival house with monthly exhibits showcasing contemporary Canadian art.

◆ The Eva Brook Donly Museum in Simcoe is a Georgian style home built in the 1840s. It now houses a local history collection and 80 works by the artist for which it is named.

◆ The Six Nations Reserve, one of Canada's largest native communities, is located north of Jarvis on Highway 6. The reserve was formed by the Six Nations (*Iroquois*, in French), native people returning to Upper Canada after fighting with the British during the American Revolution. The reserve has shops, some featuring aboriginal art. Nearby is the town of Cayuga, named for one of the Six Nations tribes.

◆ Tours are available of the Ruthven Park National Historic Site in Cayuga. The 1845 mansion is set among stone garden walls and large trees and surrounded by 1,600 acres of Carolinian Forest and farm land overlooking the Grand River.

◆ Caledonia is a charming community set beside the Canadian Heritage Grand River. The Scottish roots of its founder, Ranald McKinnon, are evident in its street names and architecture. Unique to the town is a 700-foot-long, nine-span bridge, the only one of its kind in Canada. Visit the Caledonia Mill, a restored 1913 Grand Trunk Railroad station and an 1857 town hall on Edinburgh Square. The Killman Zoo has lions and tigers and bears among its 200-animal collection.

◆ How about a little apple wine? The Northfolk Estate Winery outside the town of St. Williams at Highways 42 and 16 offers tours and tasting.

◆ Kernal Peanuts, the largest peanut grower in Ontario, is located in Vittoria. Factory tours can be arranged for groups.

◆ Selkirk Provincial Park, operated under contract by the Long Point Regional Conservation Authority, has 142 campsites, trails, a wetland walk and a beach. Haldimand Conservation Area near Selkirk, also operated by the conservation authority, has 215 campsites and nature trails.

◆ Tours are available of the authentically-decorated 1865 Cottonwood Mansion in Selkirk.

◆ Dunnville on the Grand River has campgrounds, marinas and a variety of specialty shops.

Port Dover

Sitting on the pier in Port Dover watching the fishing tugs come and go, or maybe a sea plane landing in the distance, is as much a part of the Lake Erie experience as walking the beach at Long Point. The atmosphere of this small fishing village is the reason it is a popular stop for travelers — that and the fresh perch dinners in the restaurants overlooking the lake. The town's little lighthouse at the end of a pier is an eastern Lake Erie icon. The Harbour Museum, located in a former net shed, has more than 200 artifacts from the fishing industry. Port Dover is known for its many festivals held throughout the year.

A boy walks the beach at Port Dover.

Rock Point

At the opposite end of the Haldimand-Norfolk Region's enviable Lake Erie shoreline, rocks, not sand, define the geology and set the scene for another of the most beautiful points on the entire Lake Erie Shore: Rock Point Provincial Park.

Limestone shelves embedded with fossils 350 million years old dominate the landscape, which also includes a lengthy beach and a Carolinian forest composed of shagbark hickory, black locust, blue beach and bur oak trees.

Located near Dunnville on the Niagara Peninsula, Rock Point has 129 campsites, hiking trails, swimming, picnicking and activities led by park staff such as nature hikes and campfire sing-alongs. Like Long Point, Rock Point is an excellent place to view songbirds and Monarch butterflies during migration.

A family relaxes on the beach at scenic Rock Point Provincial Park.

Bypassing the Falls

It is a feat of human ingenuity. A ship twice the length and half the width of a football field weighing as much as 1,000 loaded cement trucks travels 2,340 miles from the Atlantic Ocean to Lake Superior in just eight and one-half days. Even more impressive is the fact that the journey is uphill. Through a series of locks and canals, the St. Lawrence Seaway climbs the equivalent of a 60-story building from the mouth of the St. Lawrence River to Duluth, Minnesota, creating a web of commerce linking the North American interior with the world.

For more than 150 years, the Welland Canal has been a vital link in this chain that allows water traffic to traverse the Niagara Peninsula, bypassing the great falls. Twelve hours of the Seaway voyage is spent climbing the Niagara Escarpment in the 27-mile canal between St. Catherine's on Lake Ontario and Port Colborne on Lake Erie, where a series of eight locks gently raises the vessels 327 feet.

A ship enters one of the giant locks on the Welland Canal.

When the original canal opened in 1829, 40 wooden locks did the heavy lifting. They were replaced with 27 stone locks when the canal was widened in 1845. The third reconstruction, complete with a realignment of the northern leg of the channel and another widening, came in 1870. The present-day canal is the fourth incarnation of the waterway and opened in 1932, slicing through the center of the town of Welland.

The most significant improvement in the canal's history, including a new channel bypassing the city, was completed in 1973. The abandoned channel remains, but now serves as a waterway used for recreational boating. Merritt Island, a strip of land between the old canal and the Welland River, is also used for recreation, with biking and walking trails and historic markers that explain the significance of the canal. Two tunnels in Welland allow car, train and ship traffic to move uninterrupted at the same time.

Lock Eight at Port Colborne is one of the longest locks in the world. While Locks One through Seven do most of the lifting, it is Lock Eight's job to make the final adjustment between the water depth in the canal and the varying level of Lake Erie.

Nearly 1,000 lakers and more than 2,500 oceangoing ships, or "salties," pass through the canal each year with more than half of the traffic destined for ports overseas, especially Europe, the Middle East and Africa. Bulk cargo — grain, iron ore, coal, coke and petroleum products — make up 90 percent of the annual payload, with processed and manufactured products from lumber to heavy machinery making up the rest.

At Fountainview Park at Lock Eight, visitors can watch the parade of freighters and an increasing number of small cruise ships at the beginning or end of their journey around the falls.

Port Colborne

Port Colborne is a little lakeside community where one could easily spend a leisurely afternoon browsing the shops or sunbathing on Nickel Beach. Historic West Street is a shopping district located in century-old buildings along the canal. There is also a farmers market located in town.

The Port Colborne Historical and Marine Museum has more than 10,000 artifacts displayed in a village. For entertainment, the Showboat Festival Theatre at the Roselawn Multicultural Arts Centre stages mysteries and comedies June through September. A Canal Days Festival is held in August.

Welland

Welland, just a short side trip off Route 3 on Route 58 north of Port Colborne, has an appreciation for art and its own history. Sprinkled throughout the community are more than two dozen murals painted on the sides of buildings, each depicting a scene from the town's past, including several dealing with its namesake canal.

Welland has a central business district that includes a regional mall, several smaller shopping centers and a farmers market. It also has 42 community parks, Brock University and the Welland campus of Niagara College. Annual events include the Rose City Festival, the Heritage Folklore Festival and a Food Festival.

Fort Erie

The War began on Lake Erie in 1812 when the Americans crossed the Detroit River into Canada in an aborted bid to take Fort Malden. It ended two years later on the Niagara River at the

Earth bunkers surround Fort Erie in the town of the same name.

opposite end of the lake. Fort Erie is the site of the first and last successful American invasion of Canada and the spot where the war came to an end.

Fort Erie began as a French trading post in 1750 and was fortified in the 1760s during the Pontiac Rebellion following the French and Indian Wars (known in Canada as the Seven Years War). After twice being destroyed by ice floes, the fort was rebuilt of stone further from the river. It was blown to pieces three times by opposing forces and reconstructed each time.

The Americans captured the fort in 1813 for two weeks before retreating, only to return the following summer. The second attack was the largest — and last — invasion of Canada before the treaty that ended the war (although the largest battle would come in the American south after the treaty was signed).

Fort Erie was reconstructed in the 1930s and remains an important historic site in the history of Canada and the U.S. A collection of artifacts is housed in a museum in the 29-acre military reserve, which is open for tours in the summer. The park has field fortifications, stone walls and a monument marking a mass grave where Canadian and U.S. soldiers are buried. Reenactors bring back the drama of the bloody battle when Canada tried in vain to take back its fort during an annual Living History Week in August.

Fort Erie today is a busy little border city. It is located at the head of the Niagara Parkway, which leads to Niagara Falls, less than a half-hour drive to the north. Bridgeburg Station is the community's downtown and has a variety of shops, services and restaurants. Water is the focus of attention in Fort Erie, from the sandy shores of Lake Erie to the mighty Niagara River.

The area from Fort Erie to Niagara Falls was also a hot spot in the Underground Railroad as fleeing slaves were ferried across the river to freedom.

Area Attractions

◆ Fort Erie Racetrack is home to thoroughbred racing, including the Prince of Wales Stakes, the second jewel in the

Canadian Triple Crown. The track's park-like setting has picnic grounds, flower gardens, lakes and casual and formal restaurants. Racing is held Fridays through Sundays from May through October.

◆ The Mildred M. Mahoney Silver Jubilee Doll House Gallery has one of the largest collections of dollhouses in North America. One hundred forty exhibits span two centuries in a collection that includes rare pieces from Europe and the Orient.

◆ Fort Erie has three civic museums that offer the unique advantage of three-for-one admission: The Fort Erie Railroad Museum lets visitors climb aboard a real locomotive or caboose and tour an 1873 railroad station. It's open from Labour Day to Thanksgiving (the Canadian holidays). The Fort Erie Historical Museum, located in an 1874 town hall, houses a collection of arts, crafts and artifacts from the Neutral Indians to the United Empire Loyalists. Ridgeway Battlefield Museum commemorates an attempt by Civil War soldiers called the Finians (Irish Americans) to "liberate" Upper Canada as part of an effort to gain Ireland's freedom from Britain.

◆ The Fort Erie LaFrance Association Museum is a firefighting museum featuring a 1947 American LaFrance open cab fire truck and a 1952 ladder truck. It is open July through Labour Day. Admission is free.

◆ The Ridgeway Summer Festival is held the first weekend in July and features an antique car shop, food and music.

◆ For the gambler, Fort Erie's numerous bingo halls are open seven days a week.

◆ The largest Duty Free Shop on the U.S.-Canadian border is located near the border crossing.

Peace and Friendship

Fort Erie's annual Friendship festival, held the end of June through the Fourth of July, is a celebration of the independence and unity of the two neighbors. Music, sports, art, antique cars and an air show are all part of the festivities, which end with a fireworks display.

Like the Ambassador Bridge at Windsor, the appropriately named Peace Bridge linking Fort Erie and Buffalo is a permanent symbol of the peaceful coexistence between the two nations. And like the border crossing at the other end of Lake Erie, traffic across the Peace Bridge has grown at such a rate that a second span is in the works.

The appropriately named Peace Bridge linking Fort Erie and Buffalo is a permanent symbol of the peaceful coexistence between the two nations.

Greater Buffalo Convention & Visitors Bureau

More Information

Economic Development Corp. of Fort Erie
660 Garrison Road, Unit 1
Fort Erie, ON L2A 6E2
905-871-1332
edc@forterie.on.ca
www.forterie.on.ca

Haldimand-Norfolk Economic Development
70 Town Centre Drive
Townsend, Ontario, Canada
N0A 1S0
Tourism Inquiries:
519-426-1695
tourism.hn@sympatico.ca

Historic Fort Erie
350 Lakeshore Road
Fort Erie, ON L2A 5N8
905-871-0540

Long Point Region Conservation Authority
RR No. 3, Simcoe, ON N3Y 4K2
519-428-4623
conservation@lprca.on.ca

Point Pelee National Park
RR No. 1, Leamington ON N8H 3V4
519-322-2365

Reserve Pelee
PO Box 13
Kingsville, ON N9Y 2E8
877-867-3533
respelee@aol.com

Birding Hotlines:

Essex County Field Naturalists Club
519-966-5852

Point Pelee Migration Line
519-322-2371

CIRCLE TOUR: *Niagara Falls is about a 20-minute detour from the marked Circle Tour. Follow the Niagara Parkway north from Fort Erie to Niagara Falls, Ontario. From there you can cross the Rainbow Bridge to Niagara Falls, New York. On the U.S. side, follow the Robert Moses Parkway and the New York Seaway Trail south to Buffalo to continue the Circle Tour.*

Chapter 3

Niagara

T he tranquil ride north on the Niagara Parkway does little to prepare you for the spectacle that lies ahead. Manicured lawns stretch from the road to the front doors of country inns. Tiny boats tethered to docks scarcely move without prompting from the wake of a passing yacht. The green ribbon fringing the Niagara River from Lake Erie to Lake Ontario may just be "the prettiest Sunday afternoon drive in the world," as Winston Churchill once proclaimed.

At the town of Chippawa the water starts to stir, building to a frenzy of white foam as it reaches the rapids. Moments later, an ominous mist appears on the horizon. Anticipation builds as the traffic slows and you become mired in a jumble of cars and tour buses delivering more people to the already crowded sidewalks of Niagara Falls, Ontario.

The peaceful Sunday drive is abruptly interrupted as the river that lay so still only a few miles ago thunders over a rocky cliff into a boiling bowl below.

Above the roar of the water, the traffic and the helicopters, you cannot help noticing the voices in the crowd. Spanish, French, German, Japanese and other foreign tongues blend with countless

English dialects. Also apparent is the number of couples holding hands, beaming, oblivious to the mob around them. Niagara Falls' allure for lovers has been attributed to many things, including the aphrodisiac of rushing water. Maybe it was just good marketing, but maybe generations of newlyweds came to the Honeymoon Capital to share the memory of a sight they would never forget. Or maybe just to get lost among the distracted crowd.

In many ways, Niagara Falls is a throwback — as passe as honeymoons perhaps. But 14 million people a year still come here to experience one of the great wonders of the continent (even if it isn't really listed as one of the Seven Wonders of the World). The lure and the lore of the great falls, the rainbow, the mist and the spectacular gorge have mesmerized onlookers since the first Europeans set eyes on them more than 350 years ago.

"Incredible Waterfall"

Niagara is "an incredible waterfall which has no equal," Father Louis Hennepin declared. The French Franciscan friar who accompanied La Salle's party to the region in the winter of 1678

Niagara Falls, the Honeymoon Capital, still holds allure for couples.

Niagara Falls Tourism

***Niagara Falls plunges nearly 180
feet at the Canadian Horseshoe.***

published fanciful descriptions of what he had seen, even overesti-
mating the falls' height by four times their actual size. But who
could blame the adventurous cleric for being swept up in the
excitement?

In truth, it is not Niagara's height that makes it so remarkable.
With a plunge of nearly 180 feet at the Canadian Horseshoe and
about 100 feet at the American falls, Niagara isn't even in the top
50 of the world's tallest waterfalls. It is its breadth — the 3,600-
foot crestline — that ranks Niagara as the world's second largest
waterfall after remote Africa's Victoria Falls. Six million cubic feet
of water per minute gushes over Niagara Falls, forming the tremendous wall of water for which it is known.

The Niagara Escarpment — the steep slope over which the
water pours — was left by the last ice age when sheets of ice 3,000
feet thick carved the forerunners of the Great Lakes. The escarpment extends north as far as the Bruce Peninsula on Lake Huron's
Georgian Bay. Gradually, the Niagara River chiseled a 34-mile
path from Lake Erie to the base of the escarpment on Lake On-

tario, a 326-foot decline, half of which occurs in a single, dramatic drop at the falls.

Like the Detroit River, the Niagara is really a straight connecting two lakes (Niagara is thought to come from a native word for straight). Not far from where the river begins it divides into two channels around six-mile-wide Grand Island, New York. The streams reunite beyond the island and the river continues north uninterrupted until Goat Island splits it again, sending water over the Canadian Horseshoe Falls on one side and the American Falls on the other. The American Falls are divided once more by Luna Island, creating a third, smaller waterfall known as Luna or Bridal Veil Falls. The river, Lake Erie's only natural outlet, continues to wind through the great gorge until it empties into Lake Ontario.

Spectacular as they are, the falls today are not the same as they were when Father Hennepin first laid eyes on them. The size, shape, flow and even the location of the cliff have changed. The ceaseless flow of water has eroded the face of the cliff an estimated seven miles south from present-day Queenston, where Father Hennepin found them. The flow of the river has also been interrupted — at times cut in half — by the diversion of water above the falls. A control dam upriver funnels water into huge tunnels and canals to feed the U.S. and Canadian power plants that face each other from opposite banks downstream from the falls. The diversion of water and other controls designed to spread the flow more evenly over the crest of the falls has slowed the erosion from a rate of about three feet a year to about one foot every 10 years.

Despite all the changes since Father Hennepin became so enthralled with the falls, the priest's first impressions of the tumbling water remain more true than not. Niagara still has no equal.

The Carnival Continues

Almost as famous as the falls themselves is the carnival that surrounds them. For as long as people have been coming to Niagara, profiteers have been hatching schemes to turn a buck from the spectacle.

Even before the Erie Canal opened in 1825, providing a comfortable alternative to the bumpy nine-day stage ride from Albany, businessmen built hotels and inns in anticipation of the crowds to come. Tour boats began operating in 1818, the same year a stairway was built at the base of the cliff. By 1830, Niagara was on the route of the famous Fashionable Tours in which wealthy southerners would spend the hot months travelling between resorts in the north, while tourists of the 1850s came to the bathhouses on the American side to bathe in the "healing" waters. But the real flood came in the 1870s when railroads replaced the canal as the fastest, smoothest way to travel.

Some of the earliest promotions capitalized on the "horror" of the falls to titillate the masses, a theme that is carried over by a few dark attractions even today.

The circus began with a cruel stunt in the fall of 1927 when a small group of businessmen devised a gruesome plan to tempt tourists' morbid curiosity. The idea was to send a boat dressed up like a pirate ship sailing over the falls with a cargo of wild animals, including two bears and a buffalo. The show fell short of its promise, but the spectacle was enough to fill the taverns and hotels and begin a trend of sensational silliness.

In the summers of 1859 and 1860, dueling daredevils Blondin and Signor Farini vied for tourists' attention by defying death on

Clifton Hill is a spectacle of museums and carnival-like attractions, including a statue of Blondin balancing on a high wire over the street.

tightropes strung across the gorge. Blondin, a French actor, performed the first summer, delighting crowds of up to 10,000 with his antics 200 feet in the air. The cocky performer always found new ways to amaze spellbound onlookers, such as drinking a bottle of wine during his walk or making the 1,100-foot crossing while carrying his manager on this back.

The next year, Signor Farini strung his own line across the river starting a summer-long competition. Blondin took a stove with him on the rope walk and cooked a meal while balancing above the gorge. Signor Farini responded by carrying a wash tub, hanging his laundry out to dry on his balancing pole. The crowds ate it up; the tavern owners sat back, smiling and counting their money.

The shenanigans ceased during the Civil War, but in time the stunts would return. High wire acts came and went through 1911 as daredevils devised still more feats to amaze and delight the crowds. Others seeking fame took the plunge over the falls, a tradition that began with 64-year-old Michigan schoolteacher Annie Taylor in 1901 and has continued into modern times. A pair took the dive as recently as 1995 (they survived the drop but had to be rescued after becoming stuck on the rocks at the bottom). Fifteen people — two of them twice — have gone over the falls on purpose in barrels, boats and other contraptions, including a giant rubber ball. Five didn't live to enjoy the fame. A seven-year-old boy survived an accidental plunge in 1960.

A statue of Blondin still balances on a wire across the street on Clifton Hill, the glittering strip known for its eclectic collection of gothic museums, theaters and arcades. The Hill and other nearby tourist attractions, from viewing towers to theme parks and outlet malls, continue the carnival-like atmosphere that has besieged Niagara since the early days. But today, gambling, not high wire acts is ringing cash registers at the falls.

Casino Niagara opened in temporary quarters in 1996 with more fanfare than the coming of the Erie Canal. Since then, the region has experienced a tourism renaissance amounting to the greatest growth in its history. More than a dozen new hotels and a twin span of the Peace Bridge connecting Buffalo and Fort Erie were on the drawing board in anticipation of a larger, permanent casino opening around 2002. By then the number of visitors to the region is expected to grow to 30 million a year.

Like the promoters of the early thrill shows, hopes run high for the future of one of the most enduring tourist destinations in North America.

Viewing the Falls

It didn't take much for an early entrepreneur to make his fortune at Niagara Falls; just a fence tall enough to block the view and a ticket booth to collect the cash from tourists eager to take a peek. Today, that same businessman would probably be a parking lot tycoon.

Parking aside, you do not have to pay to see the falls. Public parks on each side of the river offer plenty of viewing areas, visitor centers and beautiful gardens. For a price, you can also view the falls from above, below and even behind the sheet of water, or from a comfortable seat in a restaurant while a waiter fetches your drinks.

Viewing the falls close enough to feel the spray.

Note that most of the water diversion from the river happens overnight, with the least interference occurring by day to preserve the beauty of the falls during peak tourist times. At night, the falls are lighted, giving visitors a reason to return after dark. The lighting schedule varies by the season. From May through August the lights remain on until midnight, while in the winter months they are turned off by 9 p.m. The Niagara Parks annual visitors guide publishes the lighting schedule.

From the Canadian Side

The Niagara Parks Commission oversees 2,888 acres of parkland containing tourist attractions, shops, restaurants and historic sites. Queen Victoria Park is the site of the public viewing areas overlooking the falls. A plaza called Table Rock House, named for a huge flat rock that once perched near the brink, is the focal point (and closest parking place).

The falls as seen from above all the commotion on the Canadian side.

The Parks Commission also operates the Great Gorge Adventure, a boardwalk overlooking the raging waters below the falls, and Journey Behind the Falls, which takes raincoat-clad visitors 120-feet down and behind Horseshoe Falls. The Niagara Spanish Aero Car is a cable car ride over the whirlpool downstream of the falls. Package rates are available to take in the falls from all of these perspectives for one rate.

The Niagara Parks People Mover, operated by the Parks Commission, is a motor coach transportation system on a 19-mile loop from just above the falls to Queenston Heights Park and back, stopping about every 20 minutes. You can ride all day for one fare, which is also included in the tour package. Six restaurants, shopping plazas and seven historical sites are also located within the park.

Many of the park's most important features lie along the Niagara Parkway, which begins at Fort Erie and stretches all the way to Fort George in Historic Niagara-on-the-Lake. A recreational trail parallels the parkway the entire 35 miles from Lake Erie to Lake Ontario. Scenes along the way include gardens, natural areas, historic sites and the power plants. The trail also has strategically located viewpoints and rest stops with picnic areas.

From the American Side

Niagara Reservation State Park, the oldest state park in the United States, surrounds the falls and takes in numerous islands as well as the Prospect Point area. From the Robert Moses State Parkway, take the American Rapids or Goat Island bridge to Goat Island where you will find plenty of parking and access to two of Niagara's most impressive vantage points. Terrapin Point, named for its turtle-like shape, allows you to stand within yards of the Falls. The best view of the Upper Rapids is from Three Sisters Island, named for the daughters of American General Parkhurst Whitney, defender of the Niagara Frontier. Luna Island overlooks Bridal Veil Falls.

There are other, more dramatic views of the falls from within the park. At Cave of the Winds you can don a yellow rain slicker and descend 279 steps to the lower gorge, coming within 25 feet of the cascading water. Observation Tower gives you a birds-eye view from 100 feet above the cliff on Prospect Point, the primary viewing area for the American Falls.

Niagara Reservation also offers a restaurant, a giant-screen theater, an open-air tour bus called the Viewmobile and the Schoellkopf Geological Museum. Packages allow you to purchase admission to all of these attractions for one price.

The Robert Moses Parkway continues along the river north from Niagara Reservation to Lake Ontario. Along the way, two other New York State Parks overlook the river and gorge. Whirlpool State Park offers views of the swirling water from two levels. Devils Hole State Park, near the Robert Moses Power Plant, also overlooks the Whirlpool Rapids and is the most popular spot on the river to fish for king (coho) salmon.

Maid of the Mist

Perhaps the most famous tour-boat operator in either the US or Canada is the Maid of the Mist Steamboat Company. The venerable tour operator has been in service since it began ferrying visitors across the river in 1846. From the deck of the boat, which

The Maid of the Mist passes Bridal Vail Falls on the American side.

***The Spanish Aero Car crosses over the
whirlpool down river from Niagara Falls.***

departs from the parks on both sides of the river, passengers
wearing rain gear pass by the Luna Falls and come close enough to
the massive sheet of water to feel the spray on their faces.

Other Options

You can see the falls from boats, double-decker buses and
helicopters, or from one of the many towers that dominate the
skyline on the Canadian side. The Minolta Tower has a restaurant
at the top. Even the casino has a tower. There are package tours
that combine, for example, boat and bus tours.

Niagara Historic Sites

In the early 1700s, the French built Fort Niagara at the mouth
of the river in what is now New York as part of a network of forts

stretching all the way to Detroit to secure the Great Lakes. When the Niagara region later became one of the original battlefronts in the War of 1812, Fort Niagara was a staging area for American troops to mount attacks across the river. In 1813, however, the British captured the fort in a campaign that also left Lewiston and Manchester (now Niagara Falls, NY) in flames. Fort Niagara remained in British hands until the end of the war the next year.

One of the bloodiest battles of the War of 1812, second only to the Battle of New Orleans, came on the night of July 25, 1813, at Lundy's Lane. It was in the final months of the war and just three weeks after the Americans captured Fort Erie. The Battle of Lundy's Lane was fought over six hours in the dark between the American army commanded by Major General Jacob Brown and the British army under Lietenant General Gordon Drummond. The fighting was fierce and unorganized. Brown's troops, the Left Division, were the best of the army and those who survived Lundy's Lane would become some of the dominant military leaders of the next 50 years. While the British rightfully claimed success at blocking the American's advancement north, Lundy's Lane, like the war itself, had no clear winner.

Today, these sites are among more than a dozen on both sides of the river where visitors can learn about the rich history of the Niagara Frontier.

American Side

◆ Old Fort Niagara has historic buildings dating from 1726. Cannon and musket firings punctuate historic reenactments staged at the fort, which also has archeology programs, military living history demonstrations and a museum. The French Castle is a focal point of the fort.

◆ Colonel Wm. Bond House is an 1824 brick house with 12 rooms and furnishings from the pre-Victorian period.

◆ Historic Lewiston is an 1820s village with shops, museums and bed and breakfast inns.

◆ Historic Lockport and Middleport are towns located on the Erie Barge Canal. The Niagara County Historical Society has a large collection of Erie Canal, pioneer, military, farming and other artifacts housed in five buildings in Lockport.

◆ Youngstown is a historic village at the mouth of the Niagara River on Lake Ontario.

The Niagara Historic Trail has erected signs throughout the Niagara region. It also publishes a brochure explaining the significance of nearly 200 historic sites along with interesting folklore.

Canadian Side

◆ Monuments and graves in the Drummond Hill churchyard mark the site of the Battle of Lundy's Lane. The Lundy's Lane Historical Museum is an 1874 cut stone building housing relics from the battle along with other historic memorabilia. Ferry Street, the oldest street in Niagara Falls, is located on the site of the battle.

◆ Fort George National Historic Site, in Niagara-on-the-Lake, is a restored 19th century military site with daily demonstrations of period blacksmithing, carpentry, musketry, cooking and music.

◆ A monument to British Major General Sir Isaac Brock, who was killed storming the heights at Queenston, stands on the Queenston Heights Park off the Niagara Parkway just past the Lewiston-Queenston Bridge.

◆ Mackenzie Heritage Printer in Queenston is the restored home and print shop of rebel publisher William Lyon Mackenzie. It contains the oldest printing press in Canada, the Louis Roy Press, one of the few wooden presses remaining in the world.

◆ The McFarland House is an example of gracious living in a Georgian mansion. Built in 1800, the house was used as a hospital in the War of 1812.

◆ Laura Secord walked 20 miles from her home in Queenston to warn the British forces of the impending attack at Beaverdam in the War of 1812. The heroine's home has been restored complete with authentic furnishings of the period.

Old Scow

One of the more interesting sights on the Niagara River is a rusting old dumping scow stranded for decades on the upper rapids. The scow broke loose from a tug in 1918 and miraculously became grounded on the rocks before plunging over the falls. It took 19 hours and the heroic efforts of Niagara daredevil "Red" Hill to save two crewmen stranded onboard. Someone had the foresight to leave the old scow right where it landed to remind us of the perils of tempting fate on the mighty river.

Niagara Attractions

You could spend a whole weekend just finding new ways to view the falls, but you would be overlooking dozens of other attractions in a region with a long history of entertaining crowds. Nightclubs, art galleries and shopping are plentiful on both sides of the border.

Canadian Side

◆ A visit to Niagara Falls would be incomplete without charging up glittering Clifton Hill for some kitschy good fun at one of the oddest collection of museums you will find anywhere. Fast food restaurants, ice cream parlors, nightclubs and miniature golf courses share the strip with Ripley's Believe it or Not, Guinness World Records, the Magical Houdini Hall of Fame, wax museums, movie theaters and haunted houses, including the House of Frankenstein.

◆ Marineland is an amusement park with roller coasters, kiddie rides and marine shows featuring dancing dolphins, killer whales and sea lions.

◆ Skylon Tower and Minolta Tower offer more than just great views. Each is a plaza of restaurants, clubs, shops and arcades.

◆ Niagara Falls Museum, near the Rainbow Bridge, is a Victorian-style building containing a large collection that includes everything from Egyptian mummies to barrels that carried daredevils over the falls.

◆ Niagara Parks Butterfly Conservatory, a relatively new attraction on the Niagara Parkway north of the falls, has more than 2,000 tropical butterflies winging freely about in a climate-controlled atrium.

Marineland amusement park has roller coasters, kiddy rides and marine shows featuring dancing dolphins, killer whales and sea lions.

Niagara Falls Tourism

◆ Floral Clock, also on the Parkway north of the falls, is just one example of the many floral attractions maintained by the Parks Commission, which has operated a school of horticulture since 1936.

◆ Dozens of wineries, farm markets and fruit groves offer tasting tours of their farms, vineyards and cellars. This is, after all, Canada's fruit belt. Many of them are on or near the Niagara Parkway, while several more are clustered along the shores of Lake Ontario near Niagara-on-the-Lake.

◆ The Niagara Peninsula Conservation Authority maintains 34 properties, including nine conservation areas, all on the Niagara escarpment. Ball's Falls Historical Park and Conservation Area, with its cascading waterfalls and 19th century buildings, is the most popular of these sites.

Casino Niagara

Since opening in 1996, Casino Niagara has been a catalyst for growth in the Niagara region. In two years, nearly 40 new developments were being discussed, including more than a dozen new hotels.

It may not look it, but the current casino, across from the Rainbow Bridge, is only temporary until the permanent Casino/Gateway complex is open in about 2002. Inside the grandiose building is an 80-foot-high glass atrium with terraced landscaping

Casino Niagara

and three-story waterfalls. The stucco glass and stone decor is reminiscent of the Great Gatsby era of the 1920s.

The casino's 96,000 square feet of gaming space offers 2,700 slot machines that accept everything from quarters to $100 bills and tempt gamblers with jackpots and prizes such as cars. High rollers will like the 144 gaming tables offering blackjack, roulette, baccarat, Caribbean stud poker, big six and other games. Stay as long as you like; the casino never closes. And if all that gambling makes you hungry, there are several restaurants, bars, lounges and a 24-hour market-style food court. The Marilyn Lounge is named for Miss Monroe, who starred in the 1953 film "Niagara" that fueled the town's reputation as the Honeymoon Capital.

American Side

◆ The Aquarium of Niagara Falls includes a large collection of Great Lakes game fish along with its marine life exhibits and shows.

◆ The Native American Center for the Living Arts is a museum of Native American history, culture, dancing, arts and crafts.

◆ Artpark, in Lewiston, is a 200-acre New York State Park devoted to the visual and performing arts. It has a 2,300 seat indoor theater with additional outside lawn seating for viewing musicals, dance and classical, pop and jazz concerts. The Castellani Art Museum on the campus of Niagara University in Lewiston is a large, marble building with a collection of 20th century and contemporary art.

◆ Rainbow mall in the heart of Niagara Falls is the center-piece of downtown. Three other malls — two of them featuring factory outlet stores — plus antique shops, art galleries and farmers markets provide enough options for a weekend shopping spree at Niagara Falls and Lockport.

◆ Niagara Power Project Visitor Center, north of the falls on the Moses Parkway, has hands-on displays and exhibits that illustrate the workings of one of the world's largest hydroelectric power plants.

◆ The Schoellkopf Geological Museum uses multimedia exhibits to explain the 420-million year geological history of the falls.

◆ The Niagara Wax Museum of History is a tribute to the daredevils that took the plunge over the falls in barrels.

More Information

Niagara Economic and Tourism Corporation
2201 St. David's Road, PO Box 1042
Thorold, ON L2V 4T7
www.tourismniagara.com

Niagara Parks Commission
877-NIA-PARK (642-7275)
www.niagaraparks.com

Niagara-USA
139 Niagara Street
Lockport, NY 14094-2740
800-338-7890
www.niagara-usa.com

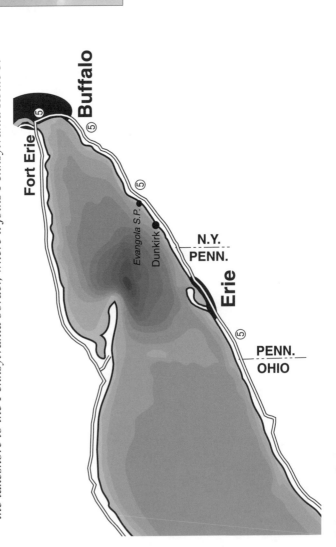

CIRCLE TOUR ROUTE: In New York, the Circle Tour follows the Seaway Trail. From Fort Erie, cross the Peace Bridge and follow the signs for New York State Route 5 south, through downtown Buffalo. Leaving Buffalo, Route 5 continues along the lakeshore to the Pennsylvania border, where it joins Pennsylvania Route 5.

Section 2

The Seaway Trail

Purple grapes dangle from green vines like jewels in a chain draped around the neck of Lake Erie's east end. Vineyards dominate the gently rolling landscape for much of the 75 miles between Buffalo, New York, and Erie, Pennsylvania. The rows of vines stretch to the white-faced bluffs that glow against the background of blue water in the early morning light.

In fall, the orange blaze of pumpkins dot the fields, and trees bordering streams cast their autumn hues on the waters where anglers wade for steelhead trout.

Route 5, as it is called in both New York and Pennsylvania, slices through the primary grape growing region of the east, traces the steps of soldiers and sailors in the War of 1812, and links two of the largest cities in each state. It is the route to fun in the summer sun, a sportsman's paradise in the fall and a winter wonderland in Lake's Erie's snow belt.

Before there was a Lake Erie Circle Tour, this route was already known as the New York Seaway Trail, a 454-mile scenic and historic route that parallels the shores of lakes Erie and Ontario and the Niagara and St. Lawrence rivers. Marked every few miles with signs depicting white footprints and waves against a green background, the route leads to quaint New England-inspired villages and fishing ports, bustling cities, wineries and farm markets, ski resorts and beaches. Designated as a New York State Scenic Biway, the route also has the distinction of being the longest National Recreation Trail in the United States.

(Note: While the Pennsylvania shore is officially designated as part of the Seaway Trail, Route 5 is marked with signs for the Lake Erie Circle Tour.)

To help make the most of the route, Seaway Trail, Inc., the non-profit organization that promotes the biway, publishes a magazine and numerous brochures and books that guide visitors to the many attractions and provide insight to their significance. Visitor information displays with large maps of the route are located in many state parks and other locations along the way.

Additional trail markers depicting a white sailing ship on a brown background identify 42 sites of significance in the War of 1812, forming a "museum without walls" and turning a pleasant drive along the scenic route into an educational experience.

Additional trail markers depicting a white sailing ship on a brown background identify 42 sites of significance in the War of 1812.

Chapter 4

Buffalo

Everything you've read about Buffalo is true. It is the snow-covered, blue-collar birthplace of barbecued chicken wings and home of a football team that is the perennial bridesmaid of professional sports. But there is also an air of dignity to New York's second largest city that is not so widely known.

Buffalo's turn-of-the-century architecture, a rich and honored history and numerous works by the impressionists hanging in the galleries of its internationally-known museum of modern art smooth out the rough edges of this industrial city. And despite what you may hear on the Weather Channel, most of the time the sun actually shines on Lake Erie's eastern shores.

The easiest way to scout Buffalo's urban terrain is to take the elevator to the 25th floor of City Hall and walk the remaining three flights to the observation deck. City streets fan out in all directions from Niagara Square 330 feet below, while in the distance ships lumber into the harbor and traffic moves swiftly west to the suburbs across the 80-foot-high Skyway.

From this vantagepoint, it is easy to see where Buffalo got its name. No, you will not see large, shaggy animals grazing in the

Greater Buffalo Convention & Visitors Bureau

The Buffalo waterfront.

fields; that buffalo probably never roamed this far east. What you will see is a "beautiful river," or beau fleuve, as the French called it and which came to be pronounced bu-ffalo. Buffalo is surrounded by beautiful waters: the Niagara River, Buffalo Creek, the Erie Barge Canal and Lake Erie.

To see the city from a different angle, venture down to the waterfront where you will find, as you might expect, a freighter taking on a payload destined for some faraway place, tugs shuttling barges upriver and pleasure boats tied up at a dockside restaurant. What you probably do not expect to find is a guided missile cruiser, but there it is, the U.S.S. Little Rock, moored right next to the destroyer U.S.S. The Sullivans and the U.S.S. Croaker submarine. The imposing scene created by the trio of naval vessels is all the more impressive because it is so out of place.

The Sullivans, named for five brothers who were among 700 American sailors killed at Guadalcanal, set sail in 1943 with a shamrock on her bow and 23 crewmen who shared the last name Sullivan. The destroyer served in World War II, the Korean War and the Cuban Blockade and never lost a man in battle. (Another ship has carried The Sullivans name since 1997.)

Naval and Military Park and adjacent Serviceman's Park dominate the Buffalo River, a widened creek that was once the western terminus of the Erie Canal. The river ends at the mouth of the mighty Niagara, forming a protected inner harbor that allows small crafts to sail right into downtown Buffalo while the freighters stay in the outer harbor.

The area between the veterans' memorials and the dome-shaped home of the Buffalo Sabres hockey team is being developed as a public plaza. Plans call for the navy ships to move upstream into a new 12-acre park with new shops, restaurants, nightclubs, apartments and offices along cobblestone streets. The Miss Buffalo, a cruise vessel that departs from a landing near the naval park, will tie up here alongside other sightseeing boats.

The Inner Harbor project, as it is called, broke ground in fall 1999 and was expected to cost $27 million. Less than a year later, Adelphia, one of the country's largest communications companies, announced plans to build a $100 million, 30-story building downtown for the company's national operations center. Plans also call for surrounding developments, such as a children's museum, ice hockey rink, retail shops, entertainment venues, residential space and a hotel. Combined, the developments will breathe new life into the history-rich city by the beautiful waters.

Naval and Military Park and adjacent Serviceman's Park dominate the Buffalo River.

Buffalo City Hall is a hulking, art deco masterpiece.

Architectural Masterpieces

Buffalo City Hall is also the place to begin a tour of Buffalo's architectural gems. The 30-story Art Deco masterpiece built in 1921 is decorated throughout with themes of pioneer life and Native American culture. The building towers over Niagara Square, the centerpiece of surveyor Joseph Ellicott's plans for the city he originally called New Amsterdam and patterned after Washington D.C. On the square is a monument to President William McKinley, who was assassinated in Buffalo in 1901.

A brochure, "Downtown's Heritage," lays out a self-guided walking tour with 38 points of interest. Among them are two of the

six National Historic Landmarks located in Buffalo: The Guaranty
Building, also known as the Prudential Building, at Church and
Pearl Streets, was built around the turn of the century from the
design of noted American architect Louis Sullivan. The steel frame
building was one of the world's first skyscrapers. Just across Pearl
street is another national landmark, St. Paul's Episcopal Cathedral,
designed by Richard Upjohn, who is said to have held the building
in higher regard than his famous Trinity Church in New York City.
The Gothic revival cathedral was built in 1849 and its spire was
completed 21 years later.

Mining more architectural treasure requires a short trip to the
city's Parkside neighborhood. There, on Jewett Parkway, is the
Prairie-style 1904 Darwin Martin House, an example of famed
designer Frank Lloyd Wright's "organic architecture" philosophy
in which a building is designed around its environment. It is
considered one of Wright's greatest works. Two other Wright-
designed houses that were originally part of the Martin estate, the
brick Barton House on Summit Ave. and the stucco frame
Gardener's Cottage on Woodward Ave., are private homes, but the
main house has been preserved for the public. They are among five
homes in Buffalo designed by the legendary architect.

With two buildings designed by Henry Hobson Richardson —
the William Dorsheimer House on Delaware Avenue and the
Buffalo Psychiatric Center on Forest Avenue — Buffalo is one of

Greater Buffalo Convention & Visitors Bureau

*Henry Hobson
Richardson, and other
famous architects,
contributed to
Buffalo's impressive
collection of buildings.*

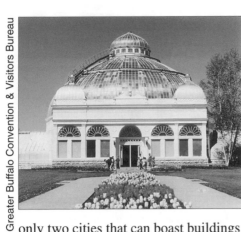

The 12-room Victorian glass conservatory at the Buffalo and Erie County Botanical Gardens is listed on the National Register of Historical Places.

Greater Buffalo Convention & Visitors Bureau

only two cities that can boast buildings designed by Wright, Sullivan and Richardson, commonly considered America's greatest architects.

The skyscrapers, church spires and monuments are not the only shapes that make up the Buffalo skyline. You also have to include the cement cylinders that were invented here in the largest flour-milling city in the world — the grain elevator.

Complimenting Buffalo's celebrated architecture is the Buffalo Park System, the first of its kind in the nation. Designed by noted landscape architect Frederick Law Olmstead, it is a series of green islands connected by tree-lined parkways that add to the gracious demeanor of Buffalo's downtown. Sprawling Delaware Park is the highlight of Olmstead's greenspaces and Buffalo's version of Olmstead's more famous creation, New York City's Central Park. A free Shakespeare festival is held here in June and July.

The Buffalo and Erie County Botanical Gardens, a 12-room Victorian glass conservatory, is situated in an 11-acre Olmstead-designed park on South Park Avenue. Built in 1890, the conservatory is listed on the New York State and National Registers of Historic Places.

Allentown: A Walk Through History

Stately stone and brick mansions along and around Delaware Avenue make up the Allentown Historic District, a reminder of

19th century prosperity when Buffalo was one of the largest cities in the United States. The neighborhood where F. Scott Fitzgerald and Mark Twain once resided is composed of well-tended homes and apartments, along with an eclectic mix of shops and restaurants. An art festival with 400 exhibitors is held here in June.

The centerpiece of the historic district is the Wilcox Mansion on Delaware Street, where Theodore Roosevelt took the oath of office eight days after President William McKinley's death in September 1901.

McKinley was on hand for the Pan-American Exposition, a convention designed to celebrate a century of progress in the Western Hemisphere. McKinley, standing in a receiving line after finishing a speech, was extending his hand to greet visitors when he was wounded by a gunshot fired by an anarchist named Leon F. Czolgosz. As McKinley lay dying, Vice-President Roosevelt was summoned from a retreat in the Adirondacks. He stayed at the home of a friend, Ansley Wilcox, and there, wearing a borrowed suit, took the oath to become the 26th president of the United States.

The Wilcox Mansion now doubles as the Theodore Roosevelt National Historic Site, one of five inaugural sites outside Washington D.C. A children's Teddy bear tea in honor of the president and Victorian decorations at Christmas are among the special events hosted at the Greek Revival home.

The New York State Pavilion on Nottingham Court across Delaware Park Lake is the only remaining structure from the Pan

The site where Theodore Roosevelt was inaugurated is a national historic site.

Greater Buffalo Convention & Visitors Bureau

American Exposition. It is now home to the collection of the Erie County Historical Society, which includes more than 80,000 artifacts, 20,000 books and 200,000 photographs about the region's history. The "Bflo Made!" exhibit features 700 products and inventions created in Buffalo, from the Pacemaker to Cheerios to kazoos.

The Erie Canal

In 1817, DeWitt Clinton, the incomparable governor of New York, pushed through legislation to begin building a 363-mile, four-foot-deep ditch connecting Lake Erie to New York City. Men as ingenious and visionary as Thomas Jefferson said it couldn't be done. "Clinton's Folly," the governor's detractors called it. Between Albany and Buffalo, there was a 573-foot difference in elevation to overcome. Surely, water can not run uphill. Besides, they quipped, who would dig the thing?

The canal would require shoveling and piling an incredible amount of dirt, clearing vast forests and removing tree roots and rock. To compensate for the difference in elevation, 83 locks and 18 aqueducts were needed. Thousands of immigrants flooded into the community to handle the backbreaking work — English, Scottish, Welch and German, but mostly young Irishmen. If Clinton's plan was folly, it was foolishness on a grand scale.

Eight years and $7 million later, Clinton led a parade of canal boats from Buffalo to New York City, where he ceremoniously — triumphantly — dumped a keg of Lake Erie water into the Hudson River. The Erie Canal, a historic feat of engineering, opened western New York and the Great Lakes region to unprecedented growth in the era between the War of 1812 and the Civil War.

"Clinton's Big Ditch," as it was called, transformed Buffalo from a small outpost on the Niagara River to one of America's great cities of the 19th century and made the Niagara region an international tourist destination. The opening of the canal also played a role in the Industrial Revolution and changed western New Yorkers' lives, from the way they made their living to what they ate for dinner.

The canal was a smooth ride compared to the stagecoach routes it replaced, but progress was hot on its heels. Just 25 years later, the canals were eclipsed by the new railroads that made the big ditches all but obsolete.

The New York State Canal System today maintains 524 miles of the former Erie and three other canals connecting hundreds of miles of rivers and lakes. Pleasure crafts now ply the waters and hikers and cyclists roam the Canalway Trail, a nearly 500-mile walking route following the towpaths across the Empire State.

In 1918, the Erie Canal was widened to accommodate larger, steam-powered boats, creating the Erie Barge Canal. At the terminus of the larger canal, where Ellicot Creek meets the Niagara River, are the Tonawandas — the cities of Tonawanda and North Tonawanda, just north of Buffalo. The Canalway Trail begins at Gateway Harbor in Tonawanda and runs, with a couple of interruptions, all the way to Lockport. Cruises and houseboat rentals are available and tour boats operate out of Lockport.

Numerous parks and buildings of the era along the canal right-of-way are reasons to visit the Tonawandas. The Herschell Carrousel Factory Museum and the Railroad Museum of the Niagara Frontier are both located in N. Tonawanda. The Historical Society of the Tonawandas maintains a museum and research center in an 1880s N.Y. Central & Hudson River Railroad station on Main Street in Tonawanda.

Museums of Art and History

Not all of Buffalo's treasures are the size of buildings and battleships. The city's public museums house everything from mummies to Monets.

◆ The Albright-Knox Art Gallery on Elmwood Avenue has a worldwide reputation for its collection of modern art, with an emphasis on American and European works of the past 50 years. Abstract expressionism, pop art and art from the 1970s and 1980s are included with works from throughout the centuries, from a Mesopotamian figure dated 3,000 BC to Andy Warhol's 1962 "100 Cans." Among the museum's permanent collection are works by Picasso, Van Gogh, Matisse, Derain, Monet and Renoir.

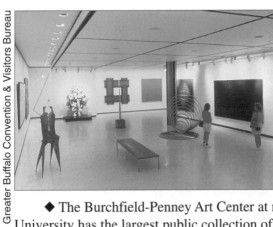

The Albright-Knox Art Gallery has a worldwide reputation for its collection of modern art.

Greater Buffalo Convention & Visitors Bureau

◆ The Burchfield-Penney Art Center at nearby Buffalo State University has the largest public collection of works by Charles E. Burchfield, who came to Buffalo in 1921 as head designer for a wallpaper company and soon devoted full time to his art.

◆ Anderson Gallery has an extensive collection of contemporary paintings, sculptures and graphics from World War II to present.

◆ The African-American Cultural Center on Masten Avenue is home to the African World Studies Archives, the Paul Robeson Theatre and the Tas'hama Children's Peer Performance Dance Group.

◆ Cofeld Judaic Museum of Temple Beth Zion is an internationally recognized museum with more than 1,000 Judaic artifacts dating from the 10th century to present. It is located on Delaware Avenue in the Allentown neighborhood.

◆ The world's largest known Kodiak specimen resides at the Buffalo Museum of Science on Humbolt Parkway, along with a Tibetan Sand Mandala and Egyptian mummies.

◆ The Mark Twain Room of the Buffalo & Erie County Public Library features a rare book collection, including the original manuscript of Twain's "Adventures of Huckleberry Finn." The five-story library is on Lafayette Square in downtown Buffalo.

The Performing Arts

The performing arts are also well represented among Buffalo's many cultural offerings. A symphony, ballet company and numerous theaters make their homes in the city's wealth of performing arts venues, many of them located in the downtown Theatre District on Main Street.

◆ The theaters in the heart of the Theater District stand out. Shea's Performing Arts Center, a 1926 European-style opera house listed on the National Register of Historic Places, plays host to touring shows, from concerts to operas to dance and children's productions. The Irish Classical Theatre Company is a new complex that preserves the works of Irish and international masters. Studio Arena Theatre, the premier resident theater for three decades, features seven mainstage and two second-stage productions per season. There is also the more intimate Pfeifer Theatre, which hosts stage performances throughout the year.

◆ Kleinhans Music Hall on Symphony Circle, which is known for its acoustical qualities, is home to the Buffalo Philharmonic Orchestra and the Buffalo Chamber Music Society.

◆ Buffalo State College on Elmwood Avenue and the State University of New York at Buffalo, North Campus, both offer centers for the performing and visual arts.

◆ Smaller venues and performing companies, some with a very specific focus, round out Buffalo's stage options. The Theater of Youth (TOY) on Franklin Street offers a full season of child-oriented performances. Alleyway Theatre at One Curtain Up Alley develops and produces new and innovative live theatre. The Ujima Theatre Company features the works by African-Americans and

Greater Buffalo Convention & Visitors Bureau

The performing arts are alive and well in Buffalo's theater district.

Thursday at the Square is a midweek distraction at Lafayette Square.

Third World artists. And the Forbes Theatre on Pearl Street is a Christian theater and home to the Promise Theatre Company. Other stages include the Kavinoky Theatre, a restored 250-seat Victorian playhouse on the campus of D'Youville College on Porter Avenue; the Buffalo Ensemble Theatre on North Jonson Park, the Paul Robeson Theater on Masten Avenue, and the Tralfamadore Cafe on Theatre Place.

Music in the Parks

Buffalo gave popular music such well-known artists as 10,000 Maniacs and the Goo Goo Dolls. The city's thriving music scene is helped by several public concerts in the summer that spotlight local performers. LaSalle Park at the foot of Porter Avenue downtown, is the site for a series of summer concerts each Tuesday and Saturday evening that brings blues, jazz, country and rock music to the waterfront. A popular music series, "Rockin' at the Knox," is held in May at the Albright-Knox Art Gallery. Another music series, Thursday at the Square, is a midweek distraction at Lafayette Square.

Big League Town

To call Buffalo a sports town would be an understatement. With major and minor league baseball, football, hockey, soccer and

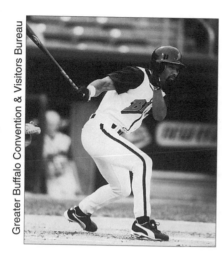

Greater Buffalo Convention & Visitors Bureau

The Buffalo Bisons baseball team is the only minor league franchise in history to draw more than a million fans for each of five seasons.

lacrosse teams, sports fans have more to cheer about than most places in the country. They also turn out to support their teams in greater numbers than in most other towns. The proof is in the stands. The Buffalo Bills, which has won four AFC championships but has never taken home a Super Bowl ring, led the National Football League in attendance at Ralph Wilson Stadium for four straight years. The Buffalo Bisons baseball team is the only minor league franchise in history to draw more than a million fans each year for five seasons. Some years, more fans pack 20,000-seat Dunn Tire Park to see the Bisons than some major league teams.

Marine Midland Arena on the Buffalo River is the center of the action in winter when the Sabres, the National Hockey League's 1996-1997 Northeast Division champs, take the ice. The arena is also home to the Bandits lacrosse team, the Blizzard professional indoor soccer team and the Destroyers arena football team. The Buffalo Wings professional roller hockey team plays at the Sports Arena at Buffalo State College.

Food and Fun

◆ About those Buffalo wings: It was the Anchor Bar on Main Street that created the barbecued chicken wing trend in 1964 as a treat for its Catholic patrons on meatless Friday nights. Buffalo wings have since become a staple of sports bars across the country,

The annual Taste of Buffalo, held in July on Main Street downtown, is one of the largest food festivals in the country.

Greater Buffalo Convention & Visitors Bureau

with as many variations on the recipe as barbecue ribs and chili. The way they do it at Frank and Theresa's Anchor Bar — that is, the original way — is with freshly ground black pepper, Frank's Louisiana Hot Sauce and a touch of white vinegar, served with bleu cheese dip and celery sticks.

◆ Buffalo may have bragging rights to chicken wings, but the suburb of Hamburg claims to be the birthplace of the burger! The story goes that the Menches brothers invented the ground beef patty there in 1885.

◆ Broadway Market is a European market with more than 40 vendors peddling ethnic delights.

◆ An Italian Heritage and Food Festival, held in July on Hertel Avenue between Colvin and Delaware Avenues, has a full midway of games and rides to enjoy between courses of Italian sausage, cannolis, tripe and calamari.

◆ The annual Taste of Buffalo, also held in July on Main Street downtown, is one of the largest food festivals in the country, bringing more than 55 local restaurants and wineries together around four stages of entertainment.

Shopping in Buffalo

◆ Buffalo's largest shopping mall is Walden Galleria, with 200 stores.

Greater Buffalo Convention & Visitors Bureau

Tifft Nature Preserve on Fuhrmann Boulevard is a 265-acre refuge within the Buffalo city limits.

◆ Main Place is a smaller shopping center with enclosed parking right downtown on Main Street between Court and Church Streets.

◆ Antique World and Marketplace in the town of Clarence, with hundreds of indoor and outdoor dealers, is western New York's largest market.

◆ Greater Buffalo also has three regional malls with more than 100 stores each: Boulevard Mall in Amherst, between Buffalo and Niagara Falls; Eastern Hills Mall in Williamsville and McKinley Mall in the suburb of Hamburg.

Parks and Nature Preserves

◆ Tifft Nature Preserve on Fuhrmann Boulevard is a 265-acre refuge within the Buffalo city limits. Part of the Buffalo Museum of Science, the five miles of nature trails, three boardwalks and 75-acre cattail marsh make the urban sanctuary an ideal place for birding, hiking and picnicking.

◆ The Dr. Victor Reinstein Woods Nature Preserve, eight miles from downtown in Depew, NY, is a 275-acre preserve that demonstrates the way Western New York looked before settlement, including 65 acres of primeval forest.

◆ The vast Iroquois National Wildlife Refuge, 40 miles from Buffalo in Alabama, New York, is nearly 11,000 acres of pristine natural area and part of the Oak Orchard Swamp. Nearby are the Tonawanda and Oak Orchard State Wildlife Management Areas.

◆ While in Buffalo, nature lovers will find it worthwhile to venture off for a day at Letchworth State Park, a great gorge known as the "Grand Canyon of the East," located about one and one-half hours away.

Buffalo Area Attractions

◆ The Buffalo Zoological Gardens, third oldest zoo in the United States, began in 1875 with a pair of deer. Today, only Niagara Falls draws more visitors in Western New York. Situated on 24 acres in Delaware Park, the zoo has 200 species of animals in its lowland gorilla/African Rainforst exhibit, Reptile House and outdoor lion and tiger "Habicat." An African predator exhibit houses rare spotted hyenas. There is also a children's zoo. Perhaps its most unique feature is not an animal, but its collection of Boehm Porcelain.

◆ Millard Fillmore, Seneca orator Red Jacket and Pony Express partner William D. Fargo are all buried at Forest Lawn Cemetery on Delaware Avenue, which is listed on the state and national Registers of Historic Places.

◆ Our Lady of Victory Basilica and National Shrine is an ornate temple built in 1926 in the 15th and 16th century Italian Renaissance style. Located on Ridge Road in the former

Greater Buffalo Convention & Visitors Bureau

The Buffalo Zoological Gardens is the third oldest zoo in the United States.

A copper dome distinguishes Our Lady of Victory Basilica.

Greater Buffalo Convention & Visitors Bureau

Bethlehem Steel town of Lackawanna, it is distinguished by its copper-topped dome and twin towers circled by angels.

◆ If you are looking for something truly unique to do while visiting Buffalo, try the tour at Q.R.C. Music Rolls, Inc., the world's oldest and largest manufacturer of player piano rolls. Historic instruments are also on display at the Niagara Street factory.

◆ On another note, take the tour at the Original American Kazoo Company in the town of Eden. Established in 1916, it is the only remaining metal kazoo factory in the world.

◆ At the Pedaling History Bicycle Museum in Orchard Park you can peruse exhibits featuring more than 300 bicycles.

Grand Island

Grand Island, a six-mile-wide island that divides the Niagara River into two streams above the falls, has a small theme park, historic sites, private campgrounds and state parks.

◆ Martins Fantasy Island has more than 100 rides, a water park, shows and a petting zoo.

◆ The River Lea Historic Farm House is a restored, furnished Victorian-style homestead featuring a collection of early-1800s memorabilia.

◆ Beaver Island State Park on W. Oakfield Road has a golf course, campground and a full range of state park amenities. Smaller Buckhorn Island State Park on East River Road is a quiet place to fish and hike. Both parks are excellent places for viewing migrating waterfowl. Big Six Mile Creek Marina State Park has a boat launch, marina and fishing access (open May - November).

The Lake Erie Snow Machine

Buffalo became known as Snow City U.S.A. because of a few newsworthy episodes including an enormous blizzard in January 1977. But while it is Lake Erie's snowiest city, in most years mere inches separate it from other cities of the region. Despite the fact that a similar blizzard blanketed the opposite end of Lake Erie just a year after Buffalo's biggest storm, nationally-televised depictions of the snowbound city have saddled it with a stereotype that is somewhat undeserved. That said, Buffalo does get its fair share of snow.

In fact, several communities along the south shore of the lake's eastern and central basins lie within a 5- to 15-mile wide snowbelt stretching from Buffalo west to approximately Lorain, Ohio. In this winter wonderland, lake-effect snow falls quickly, accumulating at a rate of up to a foot in just a few hours. These areas can receive twice the snow during a given storm as nearby

Greater Buffalo Convention & Visitors Bureau

Buffalo is Lake Erie's snowiest city.

areas just outside the snowbelt.

Three of the ten snowiest cities in the United States are located on Lake Erie's south shore. Buffalo, which averages 93 inches of the white stuff per year, is second only to Syracuse, NY, 150 miles east. Erie, Pennsylvania, ranks fourth and Cleveland ranks eighth.

Part of the credit for the piles of snow is a phenomenon known as the lake-effect, which occurs downwind of large bodies of open water when the air temperature is cold enough to form snow and the lake water is above freezing. The lake snow machine revs up as early as mid November and peaks in December, virtually shutting down after ice covers the water in mid to late January.

Buffalonians would have you know that while Lake Erie is partly responsible for the extremes in snowfall, it deserves credit also for the moderating effect it has on the climate at other times of the year. Buffalo may be known for its harsh winters, but it also enjoys gentle springs and autumns and relatively mild summers.

The New York Shore

CIRCLE TOUR ROUTE: The Seaway Trail continues on Route 5 west through Lockawanna. At Wanakah, the trail leaves Route 5 briefly to follow Old Lake Shore Drive to Silver Creek, where it rejoins Route 5.

Buffalo is barely out of sight when Route 5 slows to the pace of a country highway flanked by vast vineyards that roll with the terrain west all the way to Erie, Pennsylvania. Lake Erie is but a blur just beyond the jagged edge of the bluff. Other stretches of the lakeshore may offer more to see and do, but few compete with the grape-belt for bucolic charm.

Think of Erie as the Grape Lake. Growing grapes has been a tradition in the lake region of New York and Pennsylvania since before the Civil War. Near the turn of the century, it became an industry. That's when Charles Welch and his father, Dr. Thomas Bramwell Welch, began making grape juice, or "unfermented wine," for use in their church's communion service.

In 1897, Welch built a factory outside Westfield, New York, and later built another in the town of North East, Pennsylvania. In between are field upon field of vines bedecked with Concord and Niagara grapes used in many of the 50 products produced by Welch's, which is now a cooperative owned by 1,500 growers. In New York's Erie and Chautaqua counties alone there are more than 40,000 acres of grapes.

Grapes grown here that are not destined for the jelly jar are likely to be squeezed, fermented, bottled and corked. The Lake Erie region of Ohio, Pennsylvania and New York is one of the largest geographic areas for producing wine grapes in North America.

At the turn of the century, native American grapes were the flagships of the Lake Erie winemaking industry, with Catawba and Delaware among the most popular varieties. The advent of the modern wine industry in the 1960s saw a move toward French-American varietals, such as Vidal and Chambourcin. Since then, growers in the region have introduced Vinifera grapes, such as Riesling, Chardonnay and Cabernet Sauvignon. Today, a new generation of winegrowers is introducing cool climate viticulture and producing such varieties as Pinot Noir and Pinot Gris.

Along the Shore

◆ Woodlawn Beach State Park, west of Lockawanna, is the newest New York State Park and one of three on the Lake Erie shore. It's natural sand beach stretches for nearly a mile offering panoramic views of the lake.

◆ Evangola State Park, a short drive west near the communities of Evans Center and Angola, is situated along an arc-shaped shoreline of sandy beach edged with Angola shale. It has 80 campsites, picnic facilities, a playground, and hiking and snowmobiling trails.

◆ In Irving, where the corners of Erie, Chautaqua and Cattaraugus counties meet, Route 5 passes through the Cattaraugus Indian Reservation, nearly 22,000-acres stretching along Cattaraugus Creek. It is one of three reservations of the Seneca

New York State Office of Parks, Recreation and Historic Preservation

Evangola State Park, a short drive west near the communities of Evans Center and Angola, is situated along an arc-shaped shoreline of sandy beach edged with Angola shale.

Nation in western New York, all of which are located at least partly in Cattaraugus County.

CIRCLE TOUR: The Circle Tour leaves Route 5 to follow Lakefront Boulevard into Dunkirk before rejoining Route 5.

Dunkirk

Dunkirk, a busy little town on Chadwick Bay, sets in the heart of the grape belt. It is part of Chautauqua County, which claims more farms than any other county in New York. The county has six wineries, more than 100 roadside farm markets and is home to New York's largest Amish community. Southwest of Dunkirk are

The Dunkirk Light-house, on Gratiot Point, was built in 1875. The attached keeper's house has 11 rooms of displays of armed services and war memorabilia, and exhibits related to the lighthouse and its keepers.

Chautauqua Lake and the Victorian village of Chautauqua, a center for the arts, education, religion and recreation for more than a century.

The Dunkirk Lighthouse, on Gratiot Point, was built in 1875. The attached keeper's house has 11 rooms of displays of armed services and war memorabilia, and exhibits related to the lighthouse and its keepers. Also on the grounds is a Coast Guard and submarine exhibit room. Point Drive continues on to Point Gratiot Park, where the bluff overlooks a public beach.

A visitor center at Lake Erie State Park, west of Dunkirk, overlooks the lake from atop high bluffs. The park takes in nearly a mile of shoreline, has 97 campsites and 10 cabins, a beach and picnic shelters. It is also good spot to view migrating birds.

More Information

Greater Buffalo Convention & Visitors Bureau
617 Main Street - Suite 400
Buffalo, NY 14203-1496
Phone: 1-888-228-3369
www.buffalocvb.org

Northern Chautauqua Chamber of Commerce
212 Lake Shore Drive West
Dunkirk, NY 14048
716-366-6200
http://c1web.com/nccc

Dunkirk Chamber of Commerce
212 Lake Shore Drive West
Dunkirk, NY 14048
716-366-6200

Silver Creek Chamber of Commerce
39 Hanover Street
Silver Creek, NY 14136
716-934-2979

Westfield Chamber of Commerce
71 W. Main Street
Westfield, NY 14787
716-326-400

Fredonia Chamber of Commerce
5 E. Main Street
Fredonia, NY 14063
716-679-1565
www.fredoniachamber.org

***Worlds Apart: Fishermen at Presque Isle State Park
across the bay from Erie, Pennsylvania.***

*CIRCLE TOUR: At the state line, New York Route 5 becomes
Pennsylvania Route 5 and the signage changes from the Seaway
Trail to the Lake Erie Circle Tour. Through Erie, follow East Lake
Road, or Alt. Route 5.*

Chapter 5

Erie

The Keystone State occupies a small but enviable sliver of the Great Lakes — a 46-mile stretch between the New York and Ohio borders that is often, and accurately, described as the most scenic on the Lake Erie shore. In the center — halfway between Buffalo and Cleveland — Pennsylvania's third largest city faces its most popular state park across a bay where Commodore Oliver Hazard Perry set sail on a mission to defeat the British in the Battle of Lake Erie.

Think of Erie, the city, as a microcosm of Erie, the lake. The smallest of the big towns on the little Great Lake has significant historic sites, an impressive new waterfront district, natural areas, cultural arts, professional sports and endless recreational opportunities. Everything Lake Erie has to offer is at hand in the community that shares its name — all wrapped up in a pretty little package.

Erie is, in fact, an attractive town, the kind of place that ranks high on lists of the best cities in America to raise a family. (It placed 29th in a 1997 Readers' Digest poll.) For the 1998 film "That Thing You Do," actor/director Tom Hanks recreated Erie as it was in 1964 to depict the all-American town. The press and

Scott Historical Aerial Photos

***Erie is known as the "Gem City" because
it borders sparkling Presque Isle Bay.***

Hollywood had finally caught on to a quality of life that residents
of Erie and other communities along the lakeshore have known for
more than 200 years.

Historically, this region was part of the Erie Triangle, a
territory that once served as a military outpost for the French and
British and later became the subject of a property dispute between
five states. In what must be one of the great bargains in U.S.
history, the central government of the young country accepted
Pennsylvania's offer of 75 cents an acre to buy the Triangle in
1788. The acquisition gave the commonwealth its only port on the
Great Lakes and the start of a new industrial center.

To the millions of people who visit Presque Isle State Park, the
"Gem City," as Erie is known because of its sparkling bay, is not a
place to live or work, but to play. Pennsylvania's busiest state park
has seven miles of public beaches, walking trails, a bike path,
picnic sites and a picturesque lighthouse. The park occupies a
peninsula that curls protectively around Erie's harbor forming
Presque Isle Bay, a popular boating and fishing destination. It was
here where two-thirds of the ships in Commodore Perry's fleet
were built as the 28-year-old commander plotted the battle that

would give the United States its first advantage in the War of 1812. Perry's substitute flagship, the Niagara, returned to Erie to finish its service and was later submersed in Presque Isle's Misery Bay.

What is particularly interesting about Erie is the way its past and present seem to coexist. At a new bayfront development called Dobbins Landing, Perry's tiny warship Niagara still sails across the harbor in the shadow of the gleaming new Bicentennial Tower.

Birds-eye View of Erie

Bicentennial Tower is the best place to get the lay of the land. Built in 1995 to commemorate the town's 200th anniversary, the 187-foot structure has sixteen stations on the observation deck that provide pieces to the story of Erie's fortunate geographic location.

Station One overlooks the peninsula that forms the best natural harbor on the Great Lakes, Presque Isle Bay, which would be completely enclosed from the lake if not for a natural channel that was widened in the 1930s. The five-mile long, two-mile wide bay is 15 to 20 feet deep with a dredged shipping channel. Move your eyes east from the channel along the lakeshore and you will see the smokestacks of Erie Coke, International Paper and General Electric, the major industries on Erie's industrial east side.

Erie Area Convention & Visitors Bureau

Friendships Valhalla and Momentum sail in front of Bicentennial Tower.

Look beyond the Coast Guard Station near the channel opening to see the vast blue waters of Lake Erie and, with a little imagination, perhaps the ghosts of ships that sailed past Presque Isle long ago and were never heard from again. Due north of Erie the lake reaches its deepest point — 210 feet — in an area known for more shipwrecks than any other place in the world, including the Bermuda Triangle.

Facing the opposite direction, you can see another important geological feature of the region, the Appalachian Escarpment. The ridgeline of the mountain range south of Erie (which is sometimes visible all the way from the Ontario shore) is the southern-most boundary of the Great Lakes drainage basin. North of the ridge, the streams feed the lake; on the other side, they flow south to the Ohio River and the Gulf of Mexico. Streams like French Creek, which connects to the Allegheny River, were important to Erie's settlement because they provided a southern water route to compliment the Lake Erie port.

Following the escarpment to the lakeshore you can see the path left by the Wisconsin Glacier as it retreated north 12,000 years ago, forming the terraced terrain on which the city was built.

New and Old at the Bayfront

Bicentennial Tower is the centerpiece of Dobbins Landing, a new development at the foot of State Street in the city's historic Bayfront district. It is named for Daniel Dobbins, a well-known sailor on the Great Lakes who built the ships in Perry's fleet. Here, you can board the Presque Isle Express water taxi for an hour tour including stops across the bay at the state park, or the 149-passenger paddlewheel Victorian Princess for a sightseeing dinner cruise. The Bayfront Gallery is an artists co-op featuring locally made works of art, antiques and maritime gifts.

Bayfront Commons at the foot of Holland Street is home to the Blasco Library and the Erie Maritime Museum. The museum tells the story of the War of 1812 with multimedia and interactive exhibits and live interpretive programs. A unique display shows a recreation of the side of Perry's doomed flagship Lawrence as it would have looked after the Battle of Lake Erie. Other exhibits tell the story of the nation's first iron-hulled warship, the USS Wolverine, and changes in the Great Lakes ecosystem. Costumed interpreters bring the historical information to life.

The Brig Niagara

The museum's greatest "exhibit" is the US Brig Niagara, which carried Commadore Perry to victory over the British in September 1813 at Put-in-Bay. Perry entered the battle aboard the Lawrence under a flag emblazoned with his now-famous motto "Don't Give Up the Ship," the dying words of Captain James Lawrence, for whom the ship was named. Ironically, Perry did give up the ship, but not the battle. When the Lawrence and most of her crew were disabled, leaving only Perry and his 13-year-old brother, James, the young commander rowed to the undamaged Niagara. From the helm of the fresh ship, Perry ended the battle in a mere 15 minutes. (See chapter 8.)

Bob Lowery Photo

The US Brig Niagara carried Commadore Perry to victory over the British in September 1813 at Put-in-Bay.

The Niagara returned to Presque Isle to serve out its commission
and was scuttled in Misery Bay in 1820. To mark the 100th anniversary of Perry's victory, the city of Erie raised and rebuilt the ship
using the original keel and some of the old timbers. Towed by the
Wolverine, the ship visited ports throughout the Great Lakes,
arriving at Put-in-Bay on September 10, 1913.

In 1931, the state of Pennsylvania took ownership of the
Niagara and began an extensive renovation that was interrupted by
the Depression and finally completed in 1943. For more than forty
years it was displayed in a permanent cradle in the harbor. The ship
was totally rebuilt in 1988, incorporating some of the original
timbers in non-structural areas. It was commissioned as the flagship of Pennsylvania in 1990 and still sails to Great Lakes ports as
the goodwill ambassador of the commonwealth. When in port, the
Niagara is open for public tours.

Presque Isle

*CIRCLE TOUR: Presque Isle State Park is located next to the city
of Erie on PA Route 832. A 14-mile road loops through the park.*

The other seven Great Lake states enjoy vast and numerous
beaches, boat accesses and scenic overlooks on their shorelines.
Pennsylvania has Presque Isle. As the commonwealth's only
"seashore," the sand-lined 7 1/2-mile long, two-mile wide peninsula has been a part of Pennsylvanians' summers since even before
it became a state park in 1921.

In addition to its historic significance, the 3,202-acre peninsula is a National Natural Landmark that is home to more than 300
species of birds and 500 plants. Equally important are the dozen
beaches, 13 miles of walking trails, six boat launches and 473-slip
marina that give four million visitors a year access to
Pennsylvania's little piece of the Great Lakes.

The story of the peninsula begins 13,000 to 14,000 years ago
in the last ice age when an immense sheet of ice lumbered south
and came to rest in a valley. As it melted away, it left behind clay,
sand and gravel that formed a ridge called a moraine, while the ice
melt filled the surrounding valley with water, creating Lake Erie.

An angler enjoys great fishing on Presque Isle Bay in front of Perry's Monument.

Mark Hicks Photo

For centuries, sand accumulated along the moraine forming Presque Isle.

The evolution of the sand spit did not end there. Scientists believe that 11,000 years ago the peninsula was located about three miles west of its present location and has been moving east at the rate of about one-half mile every 100 years. The process, which has slowed over time, is the result of the longshore drift — the continual action of the waves carrying away sand and depositing it a little further east each time they sweep across the beach. During this process, some of the sand is lost. To stem this erosion, 55 breakwaters have been installed to shelter the shore, and sand is added periodically to maintain the beaches for recreation.

The best example of this succession has been seen at Gull Point, the fragile, 319-acre tip of the peninsula that has been growing for most of the last century. The point is a haven for birds to nest or rest on migratory routes that take them as far north as the Arctic Circle or south to the tip of South America. In spring, large flocks of migrating hawks and songbirds pass through here. At least three species of terns can be found at the point in warm months, while four or more species of gulls are present year round. A sixty-four acre piece of the point has been designated a natural area because of the delicate habitat that includes many endangered plant species. This special management area is closed to the public except in winter.

Presque Isle includes six distinct ecological zones, each with different plant and animal communities. They include marshes, thickets, sand plains, ponds, dunes and ridges.

Misery Bay

Misery Bay was the temporary home of Commodore Perry's fleet before the Battle of Lake Erie. Six of Perry's nine ships were built here, including two brigs, the Lawrence and the Niagara, which were made from trees found on or near the peninsula. After the battle, Perry and his men returned to Misery Bay for protection against threats of another British attack. During the winter of 1813-1814, many of the sailors died of smallpox and were quarantined at Misery Bay (hence its name). The bodies of the dead were buried there in what is now known as Grave Yard Pond.

A monument to Perry was erected in the park in 1926 at a spot called Crystal Point. The largest monument to Perry is located at the opposite end of the lake on South Bass Island where the brave young captain and his men scored their historic victory and captured an entire British fleet.

Other Park Features

◆ The beacon atop the 74-foot tower of the Presque Isle Lighthouse has warned ships away from the peninsula since 1873. The red brick house, second oldest of the American lighthouses on Lake Erie, is now used as a park residence, but the light is still maintained by the Coast Guard.

◆ The Stull Interpretive Center, near Barracks Beach, is a good place to learn about the park's natural resources and the succession of the sand spit. The Nature Shop sells books, field guides and nature-related items.

◆ Presque Isle is located on the Atlantic Flyway for migrating birds and is widely considered one of the best birding locations in the United States.

Benjamin E. Carter Photo

***Presque Isle
Lighthouse***

◆ Several beaches are guarded from Memorial Day through Labor Day. Four of them have beach houses with restrooms and changing facilities. Beaches range from secluded picnic areas to large recreation areas with volleyball courts. Waterworks Beach has wheelchair access to the water's edge. Sunset Point is a popular area for kite flying and windsurfing.

◆ Presque Isle is naturally popular with fishermen, who angle for smelt, perch, bass, walleye, trout and salmon on Lake Erie and everything from panfish to northern pike to muskellunge in the

***Presque Isle State Park
offers miles of excellent
swimming beaches.***

bay. Bowfishermen stalk the channels and marshes. Boats may be rented at a concession at Grave Yard Pond.

◆ Ice boating, cross-country skiing and ice skating on Misery Bay are popular winter activities. Unique features in winter are the ice dunes formed by the combination of lake ice, wave surge and freezing spray. The Erie area is part of the Lake Erie Snow Belt.

◆ Other popular recreational activities include canoeing, SCUBA diving, water skiing and hunting during special controlled hunts.

Downtown Erie

Imagine theexcitement that the opening of the Warner Theatre must have stirred during the Great Depression. The grand theater named for the Warner Brothers motion picture studios opened in 1931 and promised to bring the "pick of the major film releases." That it did, plus traveling shows including the vaudeville acts of the time. The art-deco movie house, trimmed with gold-backed mirrors, crushed velour and silver and gold leaving, still hosts

Erie Area Convention & Visitors Bureau

Actors perform at the Erie Playhouse.

*Historic architecture, like the Erie County
Courthouse, is part of Erie's character.*

traveling shows, including national Broadway touring productions.
Now called the Warner Theatre Center for the Performing Arts, it is
home to the Erie Philharmonic, one of the oldest symphony
orchestras in the nation, and the Lake Erie Ballet Company.

Discovery Square, in the block bounded by State and French
Streets and Fourth and Fifth Streets, is a center for history, science
and art. The renovated square includes the Erie History Center and
Society for Genealogical Research, and the Erie Art Museum,
which is located in the Old Custom House on State Street, an
elegant Greek Revival building built in 1839 as a bank. The Square
is also home to the ExpERIEnce Children's Museum, a hands-on
education and recreation center where you'll never hear anyone
say, "don't touch." Natural, social and physical science exhibits
encourage children to explore with all of their senses.

The Dickson Tavern on French Street is the oldest surviving
building in Erie. It is furnished as a 19th century tavern. The
Cashier's House, also on State Street, is listed on the National
Register of Historic Places.

Other Erie Historic Sites

◆ General "Mad" Anthony Wayne, commander of the Legion of the United States and hero of the pivotal Battle of Fallen Timbers near present-day Toledo in 1794, is buried in Erie — sort of. In 1809, the general's son came to exhume his father's body from a grave at Fort Presque Isle with plans to return the bones to the family cemetery in Radnor, Pennsylvania. When he found the body was still too well preserved and too large to transport by horse, the son arranged to have the flesh re-interred in the original grave and took the bones home. That makes Wayne the only US hero to be buried in two places at the same time.

◆ Wayne's blockhouse, a reconstruction, commemorates the colorful general. It sets on the site of the French Fort Presque Isle on the grounds of the Soldier's & Sailor's Home at East Second and Ash streets.

◆ The Firefighters Historic Museum on Chestnut Street is an old firehouse with displays of antique firefighting apparatus, complete with a 1920 LaFrance pumper.

◆ The Historical Museum on the campus of Gannon University on West Sixth Street has displays about the Battle of Lake Erie and local and maritime history.

◆ There are four covered bridges in the region each built between 1868 and 1875. Harrington Bridge on LR 225088 and Carmen Bridges on TR 338 both cross Conneaut Creek near the Ohio border northeast of Cherry Hill. There is also the Gudgeonville Bridge over Elk Creek, southeast of Girard on TR 460, which was named for a mule, and the Brotherton Crossing Bridge over LeBoeuf Creek east of Waterford on Niemeyer Rd.

Other Erie Area Attractions

◆ The Erie Zoo and Botanical Garden of Northwest Pennsylvania has more than 300 animals including a white Bengal tiger, an otter exhibit and African wild birds. It also has a children's zoo and sightseeing train rides.

Erie Area Convention & Visitors Bureau

***Waldameer Park & Water World is located
at the entrance to Presque Isle State Park.***

◆ Waldameer Park & Water World is a popular amusement park at the entrance to Presque Isle State Park that has been drawing summer fun-seekers for more than a century. The park has 75 rides, waterslides, pools, a midway arcade and picnic areas. There is no charge for parking or admission. Tickets may be purchased for the rides. The park is closed Monday except on holidays. A campground is located across the street.

◆ Besides the Presque Isle Lighthouse, there are two other beacons in Erie. The Land Lighthouse at the foot of — naturally — Lighthouse Street on the east side of town was built in 1867, continuing a tradition of lighthouses on the spot dating to 1818. The North Pier Lighthouse is located at the entrance to the channel at Presque Isle.

◆ Erie Playhouse on West 10th Street. is one of the largest community theaters in the country and hosts plays, musicals, comedies and a youth theater.

The grape is King in North East, Pennsylvania, home of the North East High School "Grapepickers." The town is also home to the Penn Shore Winery and Vineyards and Mazza Vineyards, both of which offer tours and wine tasting.

North East, Pennsylvania

The vineyards that blanket the hills in New York roll on into North East, Pennsylvania, home of the second Welch's processing plant and the North East High School "Grapepickers." The town is home to the Penn Shore Winery and Vineyards and Mazza Vineyards, both on East Lake Road. The wineries offer tours and tasting. North East hosts the Wine Country Harvest Festival in September. There are two other wineries in Erie County: the Heritage Wine Cellars and the Presque Isle Wine Cellars.

Sports

Erie has two minor league sports teams: The Erie SeaWolves is a AA affiliate of the Anaheim Angeles baseball team. The SeaWolves play at Jerry Uht Park next to the Erie Civic Center, home of the Ontario Hockey League's Erie Otters.

Shopping

Perhaps the second biggest attraction in Erie, after the state park, is shopping. Shoppers from Ohio and New York cross the border to buy clothing, which is exempt from sales tax in Pennsylvania.

The largest shopping center in northwest Pennsylvania is Erie's Millcreek Mall. The regional mall has more than 200 retail shops and is surrounded by a growing number of shopping plazas and "big box" stores in a section of town called the Uptown Shopping District.

Festivals

We Love Erie Days in August and the Erie Summer Festival of the Arts at the end of June are large annual festivals in Erie. The city also holds a First Night Celebration on New Year's Eve. The town of North East is known for its Cherry Festival each fall,

Nearby

Routes 6 and 6N south of Erie make up the Army of the Republic Highway. The roads intersect at the town of Waterford, where there stands the only statue of George Washnington in British uniform.

Erie Wildlife Refuge

The Erie National Wildlife Refuge, 35 miles south of the lakeshore in Crawford County, has about 9,000 acres in two units. French Creek, the most biologically diverse stream in the state, runs through the refuge and contains more than 80 species of fish.

Terry Way Photo, U.S. Fish & Wildlie

A pond in the 9,000-acre Erie National Wildlife Refuge, 35 miles south of the lakeshore in Crawford County.

Three distinct habitats — forest, field and water's edge — are here, along with 47 species of mammals, 237 species of birds, 37 amphibians and reptiles, and several rare freshwater mussels.

The Sugar Lake Division of the refuge, 10 miles east of Meadville on the outskirts of Guys Mills, is home to two streams, beaver ponds, pools and marshland. The smaller Seneca Division is about 10 miles north (four miles southeast of Cambridge Springs) and is known more for its wetland habitat.

CIRCLE TOUR: West of Erie, the Circle Tour leaves Route 5 and follows US 20, which crosses the Ohio border.

Girard

◆ Girard, PA, est. 1846, on Route 20, was home to America's most famous clown in the 19th century. Dan Rice, who lived from 1823 until 1900, made Girard the winter quarters for his traveling circus from 1856 until 1875. Harper's Weekly used Rice's likeness as the basis to create Brother Jonathan, a character that later became an American icon known as "Uncle Sam." The town still hosts a summer festival in Rice's honor.

Girard has two museums depicting life in the 1800s:

◆ The Hazel Kibler Museum of Local History on East Main Street has Dan Rice memorabilia, a large collection of toys once made by a local manufacturer, and revolving displays.

◆ The Battles Museum of Rural Life is located on 130 acres of woods and farmland. It is actually composed of several buildings, including the Battles Bank Museum on Main Street.

◆ A Civil War monument in the center circle of the borough was the first such monument to those who died in the conflict.

Rolling west from Erie, the bustle of the city quickly fades and the countryside reappears. A fishing access on Elk Creek is a scenic spot for one last stop before the Ohio border.

Due south of West Springfield, on the Ohio-Pennsylvania border, a flood-control reservoir created on the Shenango River forms the largest inland body of water in Pennsylvania, Pymatuning Reservoir. There are popular state parks on each side

The Elk Creek Access is a pleasant spot on the Pennsylvania shore just before the Ohio state line.

of the state line, both named for the reservoir that straddles the boundary.

More Information

The Erie Area Chamber of Commerce
109 Boston Store Place
Erie, PA 16501
(814) 454-7191
www.eriepa.com

Presque Isle State Park
P.O. Box 8510
Erie, PA 16505
814-833-7424
www.dcnr.state.pa.us/stateparks

Girard-Lake City Chamber of Commerce
Post Office Box 118
Lake City, PA 16423
814-774-3535
http://girard-lakecity.com

Pennsylvania Wine Association
PO Box 2304
Sinking Spring, PA 19608
www.pennsylvaniawine.com

CIRCLE TOUR: Entering Ohio: Shortly after US 20 crosses the Ohio border; the Circle Tour jogs to the north, following Ohio Route 531 along the lakeshore through Conneaut, Ashtabula and Geneva-on-the-Lake. The route turns south on Ohio 534 and rejoins US 20 west in Geneva. At Painesville, it follows Ohio 535 to Ohio 283 and continues west to Cleveland.

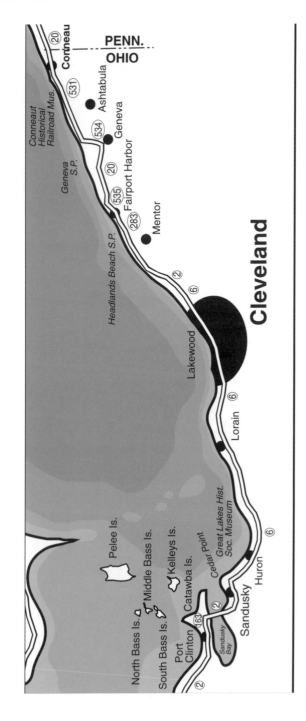

Section 3

Ohio's North Coast

Most of northern Ohio looks very different from this corner of the Buckeye State, which more closely resembles the Pennsylvania landscape thanks to the Allegheny Plateau. The northwest corner by contrast is flat as a board and covered with soybeans, wheat and corn. Such is the diversity along Ohio's 240-mile share of Lake Erie's south shore, which is longer than the shores of New York, Pennsylvania and Michigan combined.

The North Coast stretches for three-quarters of Ohio's northern border, through two of the state's largest cities and one of its most popular vacation regions. Along the way is the largest fleet of sport fishing charter boats on the Great Lakes, two nuclear power plants, giant auto foundries, cavernous sports stadiums, family farms, nature preserves and more roller coasters than you'll find anywhere else in the world.

Our journey begins in the northwest corner — Ashtabula County — where carousel music still drifts on the cool lake breeze and covered bridges still offer refuge from a spring cloudburst to anyone who happens to be traveling on horseback.

A gull rests on a dock in Ashtabula.

Just a few miles away, the pace picks up as Cleveland comes closer and pastoral scenes give way to the manicured lawns of suburbia and a frenzied race for the city. Linger awhile in Lake County and you'll find a comfortable compromise. Ohio's smallest county has the state's longest beach, the nation's largest arboretum, a miniature Napa Valley wine district and a president's home.

Northeast Ohio has a history of being set apart from the rest of the state. It belonged to the Western Reserve, a 120-mile long, 75-mile wide tract of land claimed by Connecticut after the Revolutionary War. When other colonies conceded their western land holdings to the federal government, Connecticut was allowed to reserve a section from the Pennsylvania border to Sandusky Bay as a place where its residents could start over after the war. The 18th Century New England influence is obvious even today in the architecture sprinkled throughout the region from quaint Painesville to downtown Cleveland's Public Square.

The region remained a colony of the New England state outside the jurisdiction of the federal government's vast Northwest Territory, but the threat of hostile Indians kept the Western Reserve from being settled until the Battle of Fallen Timbers near present-day Toledo in 1794. Within a couple of years of the battle, northeast Ohio was on its way to becoming one of the major trading regions in the young United States.

For more information about the counties along Ohio's share of the Lake Erie Circle Tour, go to www.circle-erie.com

The 16 covered bridges in Ashtabula County, Ohio were built between the 1860s and 1990s, the most recent one in 1999.

Chapter 6

The Northeast Corner

A covered bridge on the countryside conjures up romantic notions of a simpler time. It represents the ingenuity and kindness of strangers who left it behind for the comfort of some future traveler. What does this say, then, about Ashtabula County, Ohio, which not only has preserved covered bridges for more than a century, but it continues to erect the charming spans to this day?

The county's 16 covered bridges were built between the 1860s and 1990s, the most recent one in 1999. Among them is the Windsor Mill Covered Bridge over Phelps Creek, a national historic site, the Harpersfield Bridge spanning the scenic Grand River, which is the longest covered bridge in Ohio — even a covered bridge converted to a pizza parlor. Plans are now on the drawing board to build the longest covered bridge in the world.

These trestles are more than a quirky character trait for this rural county in Ohio's northeast corner, they are a tourist attraction drawing an estimate 25,000 people a year. The largest crowds come during the annual Covered Bridge Festival the second weekend of October at the Ashtabula County fairgrounds in Jefferson.

Ohio's northeast corner is an easygoing place where vineyards and nurseries blanket the rolling terrain that greets visitors at this scenic gateway to Ohio's Lake Erie shore. Five a.m. might be considered rush hour in Conneaut, Ohio's northernmost port, as fishermen make their way to Conneaut Creek to wade for steelhead on a cool autumn morning or head for the harbor in pursuit of central basin walleye or yellow perch.

A bridge from another era traverses Ashtabula Harbor. The 1925 Bascule Lift Bridge, one of six in the United States, still raises and lowers 24 hours a day as needed for the ships and pleasure craft that pass through the busy port. Bridge Street, a row of antique shops, restaurants and other stores, has been restored to the grandeur of the late 1700s, only without the rowdiness for which this harbor town was once known.

The Great Lakes Marine & U.S. Coast Guard Memorial Museum on Walnut Boulevard occupies a building that once housed two lighthouse keepers who took turns standing watch. In 1984, it became a museum and now holds hundreds of Great Lakes artifacts including model ships, a wheel from a steamer, photographs, a working model of one of the Welman Electric Huletts and a working radar unit.

Ashtabula County has many historical sites and museums that document how the people of an earlier century lived and worked. Geneva-on-the-Lake is a living example of how they played. At Ohio's oldest summer resort, visitors today can travel back 125 years to a simpler time in a one-mile stretch known as "The Strip."

Ashtabula Harbor is a busy boating center in northeast Ohio.

Cullen Spencer and Edwin Pratt opened the Sturgeon Point amusement park on the Fourth of July in 1869. Summer cottages sprang up as the park gained popularity as a summertime vacation destination. In the early 1900s, dance halls like the Casino and the Pier Ball Room welcomed the likes of Glen Miller, Duke Ellington, the Dorsey Brothers and Tommy Tucker. Later, Guy Lombardo, Lawrence Welk and Perry Como began their careers at the popular Geneva-On-The-Lake resort dance hall, which closed in 1973.

The mile-long Strip that evolved from Sturgeon Point remains. Visitors can still plink targets in a shooting gallery, try their luck at an antique pinball machine, or just putt around at the oldest miniature golf course in the country. For a treat, they can pop in to one of the restaurants on the street, or snack on shaved ice and popcorn. While Sturgeon Point is long gone, Erieview amusement park, with rides and waterslides, keeps the 125-year-old summer tradition alive.

More Historic Sites

◆ The Conneaut Railroad Historical Museum in a former New York Central depot at 324 Depot Street has a fascinating collection of railroad records and memorabilia, as well as actual rail cars and steam engines.

◆ The Hubbard House on Walnut Boulevard at Lake Avenue was built in the 1830s and was a station on the Underground Railroad. Now a museum, it is open weekends for tours.

◆ The Jennie Munger Gregory Museum, an 1823 farmhouse in Geneva-on-the-Lake, is the headquarters for the Ashtabula County Historical Society. The two-story home's 14 rooms are loaded with history — clothes, furniture, pictures, and memorabilia. Whole rooms are furnished in late Victorian style.

◆ The collection in Shandy Hall in Geneva has the belongings of generations of the Harper family that lived there for 120 years. Colonel Robert Harper built the 17-room-home in 1815 following his service in the War of 1812. It is one of the oldest remaining homes in the Western Reserve.

◆ One of the most unique historical collections you will find is the Victorian Perambulator Museum in Jefferson, which features a collection of more than 150 wicker baby and doll carriages from 1860 through 1910. It also has pre-1900 children's items such as sleighs, dolls, velocipedes, farm wagons, toys, books, games and pictures.

Geneva State Park

Geneva State Park, on Ohio 534 north of the town of the same name, is a 698-acre natural area that affords the best public access to Lake Erie in the region. Its sandy beach is the length of three football fields and is a popular spot for sunning and swimming. The beach takes a beating from the lake, although numerous shoreline protection devices have taken some of the punch out of the merciless assault.

Geneva's 91-site campground, cabins, picnic areas, 383-slip marina, boat launch and transient docks make it an attractive and busy spot for lake lovers. Information about fishing aboard one of the many charter boats that operate out of the marina is available at the marina store. Fishing is also permitted along the breakwall that protects the marina. Like all 74 Ohio State Parks, Geneva is open free of charge 6 a.m.-11 p.m. Some facilities within the parks, such as beaches and concessions, have separate hours.

The Lake County Countryside

The most distinctive features of northeast Ohio are the nurseries, orchards, farm markets and wineries along its rolling country roads. Lake County has been known for more than 100 years as one of the best regions in the country to grow nursery stock and fruit because of Lake Erie's moderating effect on the climate. Concentrated in a belt six to ten miles wide and running through Willoughby and Madison are at least 115 nurseries. Lake County Nursery in Perry is one of the largest wholesale nurseries in the US, with more than 1,000 acres. The Borlin Florist & Greenhouses in Mentor is Ohio's largest grower of orchids.

Lake County Visitors Bureau

Visitors enjoy an outing at at Chalet Debonne Vineyards in Madison where wine is aged in oak barrels made from trees felled on the family farm.

Wine is aged in oak barrels made from trees felled on the family farm at Chalet Debonne Vineyards in Madison. Northeast Ohio is a mini-Napa Valley wine district, with about a dozen wineries from Conneaut to Cleveland.

In Geneva, they celebrate the fruit of the vine with an annual two-day Grape JAMboree in late September. Three times Lake County has also hosted the annual Vintage Ohio wine festival, organized by the Ohio Wine Producers' Association.

Holden Arboretum

With a nationally significant arboretum, a first rate Metropark district, a popular state park and two state nature preserves, Lake County is obviously a community that treasures its natural areas. Holden Arboretum in Kirtland is a 3,100-acre preserve of display gardens, horticultural collections and more than 20 miles of nature

Lake County Visitors Bureau

Holden Arboretum in Kirtland is a 3,100-acre preserve.

trails. The largest arboretum in the United States, the facility is a year around attraction and a place for serious study. The Horticulture Science Center is a state-of-the-art facility where woody plants are grown for research, conservation and collections. Holden is a 7,000-member organization engaged in horticultural research, plant collection and management, education and interpretation. Its more than 8,000 varieties of trees constitute one of the world's largest collections.

Lake Metroparks

Lake Metroparks, a national award-winning park district, has 20 parks and 12 nature preserves totaling more than 5,000 acres, mostly along the Grand River and two of its tributaries. On the lakeshore, the park district operates Lakeshore Reservation in Madison, which has a sculpture garden; Painsville Township Park, which has a community center and dance hall; Fairport Harbor Lakefront Park, which has a beach, and the Erie Shores Golf Course in Madison.

Penitentiary Glen Reservation in Kirtland is located in a steep, nearly inescapable gorge from which it takes its name. The park features hiking trails, a nature center, classrooms, a wildlife rehabilitation center and picnic areas.

Lake Farmpark in Kirtland, once voted the best park in America, is the park district's most unique facility. It is an open-air science and cultural center, a farm animal petting zoo, an agricul-

Lake County Visitors Bureau

Lake Farmpark in Kirtland, once voted the best park in America, is the park district's most unique facility.

tural demonstration facility and host to numerous annual events, including a Christmas light display. Here, kids can milk a cow and learn that their food doesn't come from the supermarket.

Presidential Digs

James Garfield is remembered more for his presidential campaign than his presidency — but then the campaign probably lasted longer. Just four months after being elected the United States' 20th chief executive in 1881, the northeast Ohio native was assassinated by a gunman in a Washington, DC, railroad station.

Garfield was a legend in the Cleveland area long before that final election. A Cuyahoga County native, he worked on the massive Ohio and Erie Canal project, rose through the ranks to major-general in the Civil War and later became president of his alma mater, Hiram College. His election to Congress in 1863 began a 17-year run as the representative of the people of northeast Ohio. He was elected to the U.S. Senate in 1880, but before he could take office, the radical Republican was nominated as a compromise candidate for president.

Garfield is perhaps best known outside Cleveland for his unconventional presidential campaign. Rather than traveling the country he conducted a "front porch" campaign, meeting dignitaries at his Mentor home he called Lawnfield.

Lawnfield, now called the James A. Garfield Historic Site, pays tribute to Garfield, one of seven Ohioans to hold the office of president.

Carl A. Stimac Photo

Today, Lawnfield pays tribute to Garfield, one of seven Ohioans to hold the office of president. Now called the James A. Garfield Historic Site, the 30-room estate includes original furnishings owned by the Garfields, as well as a replica of the log cabin in which the president was born. The historic site underwent a $15 million renovation in 1994.

Garfield is buried at Lakeview Cemetery on Euclid Avenue and E. 123rd Street in Cleveland, his grave marked by a 120-foot monument.

Other Historic Sites

◆ The Old Tavern in Unionville is said to be the oldest building in Ohio. It was built in 1798 as a stagecoach stop. During Abolition, it was a station on the Underground Railroad. Today it is a dinner theater.

◆ Rider's Inn in Painesville was an 1812 inn on the stagecoach route between Buffalo and Cleveland. It is now a bed and breakfast and full service restaurant.

◆ The Little Red Schoolhouse in Willoughby is a one-room school with authentic furnishings that teaches children about the period from 1900 to 1930 through demonstrations and hands-on activities.

◆ Kirtland Temple Historic Site in Kirtland is the first church build by the followers of Joseph Smith, founder of the Latter-day Saints movement, when they moved to the Western Reserve in the

Lake County Visitors Bureau

The Old Tavern in Unionville was part of the Underground Railroad. Today it is a dinner theater.

Kirtland Temple Historic Site in Kirtland is now owned by the Reorganized Church and listed as a state and national historic landmark.

1830s. Now owned by the Reorganized Church, it is listed as a state and national historic landmark. The church also operates Newell K. Whitney Store and Historic Site, a museum and store awarded the President's Historic Preservation Award in 1988. It is located near the church.

♦ Indian Museum of Lake County, on the campus of Lake Erie College in Painesville, houses prehistoric Ohio artifacts dating from 19,000 BC to 1650 AD, many of which were excavated at a local site.

♦ The Lake County History Center and Museum, located on 15 wooded acres atop Little Mountain in Mentor, is a collection of historic buildings including a one-room school, log cabin and a pre-Columbus Indian camp. The museum, housed in a former estate, features items from the area's agricultural past.

♦ Coulby Mansion and Wickliffe City Hall in Wickliffe has a huge entrance gate leading to the foyers, fireplaces and halls of this 16-room mansion built with Italian marble.

♦ Mooreland Estate in Mentor is a Victorian mansion preserved by Lakeland Community College.

♦ The Aviation Museum, located in the Shoregate Shopping Center in Willowick, is a United States Aviation Museum Annex that displays aviation related shirts and caps, a restored World War II Link Trainer and other aviation related items.

Fairport Harbor

The serpentine paths of the Chagrin and Grand rivers etch beautiful valleys through Lake County's rolling terrain. The point where the rivers finally reach their destination provides a precious commodity in northeastern Ohio — access to Lake Erie. Unlike the lake's western basin, where the land lies almost even with the water, bluffs as high as 70 feet form a cliff along the central basin. Because of this barrier, the mouths of these two state Scenic Rivers are popular places.

Fairport Harbor is a recreational and commercial harbor where pleasure boats cross paths with ships and barges carrying sand, gravel, limestone and rock salt. Marinas are plentiful in the villages of Fairport Harbor, on the east bank, and Grand River, on the west bank.

Grand River has a U.S. Coast Guard Station. It also has the beginnings of a restaurant and tavern district and is the site of a Perch Festival in September.

The Fairport Marine Museum in Fairport Harbor is partly housed in a former lighthouse. The 60-foot tower and beacon was a guiding light not only for ships, but for runaway slaves traveling the Underground Railroad under cover of night. Another part of the museum is housed in the pilothouse of the Great Lakes Carrier

"Frontenac." The national historic landmark, which sets atop a bluff overlooking the harbor, was the first Great Lakes lighthouse marine museum and contains a collection of Great Lakes shipping memorabilia.

Winding rivers etch beautiful valleys through the rolling terrain of northeast Ohio.

Lake County Visitors Bureau

***The Fairport Harbor
Lighthouse.***

2,000 Feet Under The Lake

Large piles of rock salt on the west bank of the harbor tell part
of a fascinating story of an important but little known Lake Erie
resource. The Morton Salt Co. mine in Grand River stretches 2,000
feet below Lake Erie to huge salt, or halite, beds left by glaciers
more than 410 million years ago. The salt is excavated in large
solid blocks creating salt "rooms" with massive pillars between
them to support the mine. It is estimated that these salt beds are so
vast that if mined at their current rate they would last 32,000 years.
Because of the Morton mine and the International Salt Mine at
Whiskey Island in Cleveland, Ohio ranks among the nation's top
producers of rock salt used to melt snow and ice on roadways and
for industrial applications.

Headland Beach and Dunes

Just west of Grand River, State Route 44 ends at the entrance
to Headlands Beach State Park. Headland Beach and it's neighbors, Headland Dunes and Mentor Marsh state nature preserves,
combine to form an important complex whose attributes are
apparent by their names: beach, dunes and marsh.

Headlands Beach is a mere 125 acres, but within this small
park is the largest natural beach in Ohio — a 150-yard wide band

Headlands is Ohio's largest natural beach.

Lorain County Visitors Bureau

of sand that stretches for a mile. The soft sand, rolling waves and beautiful vista attract more than a million visitors a year.

Headland Dunes State Nature Preserve at firsts looks like just another part of the state park. The 16-acre preserve is accessible from the park and separated from it only by a snow fence to contain the blowing sand. Headland Dunes is one of the best — and last — of the beach dunes in Ohio, a Great Lakes version of the type of shoreline community found along the Atlantic Coast and including many of the same rare plants. Some of the plant species found here cannot be found further inland, and many are unique even to this corner of the state. Headland Dunes is also an excellent place to view migrating birds and Monarch butterflies in autumn.

The Buckeye Trail, a 1,200-mile hiking trail that generally follows the Ohio state boundaries, runs through the state park and nature preserve.

Mentor Marsh State Nature Preserve, on Corduroy Road just south of the state park, is a 647-acre marsh owned by The Cleveland Museum of Natural History. It became one of the first properties in Ohio to be protected by the Ohio Department of Natural Resources, Division of Natural Areas and Preserves. Mentor Marsh is an ancient riverbed of the Grand River that is home to a large variety of wildlife such as beaver, deer and owls thanks to its diversity of habitat. Five trails, ranging from 0.1 to 2 miles in length, take hikers to forests, meadows, shallow ravines and scenic overlooks.

Other Attractions

◆ Gallery One in Mentor is said to be the largest art gallery in the United States, featuring more than 30,000 pieces for sale.

◆ Lake County has 27 public and private golf courses. Quail Hollow, at the intersection of I-90 and Ohio Route 44, is Ohio's only AAA Four-Diamond golf resort. It has two 18-hole courses and is host to the Nike Cleveland Open.

◆ The Boulevard of Flags at Eastlake City Hall has 500 American flags, the largest permanent display in the United States.

More Information

Ashtabula County Convention and Visitors Bureau
1850 Austinburg Road
Austinburg, OH 44010
800-337-6746
accvb@accvb.org
www.accvb.org

Lake County Visitors Bureau
1610 Mentor Avenue, Room 2
Painesville, OH 44077
800-368-5253
www.lakevisit.com

Lake Metroparks
11211 Spear Road
Concord Township, OH 44077
800-277-7275
www.lakemetroparks.com

Ohio Wine Producers Association
P.O. Box 157
Austinburg, OH 44010
www.ohiowines.org

Louie Anderson Photo (computer modified)

The Flats, Cleveland's lively night club district, replaced dilapidated warehouses and piles of iron ore along both banks of the lower Cuyahoga River.

CIRCLE TOUR: The Circle Tour continues west on Ohio 283 (Lake Shore Boulevard) through Eastlake, Willowick and Euclid, then follows Ohio 2/I-90 through Cleveland.

Chapter 7

Cleveland

T his always happens," the cab driver grumbles, lament
ing what he sees as a slow April evening following an
Indians defeat earlier in the day. "When they lose, I
lose." Had it been an evening game — and a victory for the Tribe
— the dining and drinking establishments that make up The Flats
would be overflowing with frenzied fans, he said. This night, the
place is merely packed.

The crowd is already so large it's hard to believe you could fit
one more bobbing body into the Howl at the Moon Saloon at the
Nautica Complex where dueling piano players are creating a
frenzy of their own. Throngs of people is something to be taken for
granted at The Flats, Cleveland's lively night club district that
replaced dilapidated warehouses and piles of iron ore along both
banks of the lower Cuyahoga River.

That any city these days has the magnetism to pull people
downtown from the suburbs after dark is impressive. That it is
Cleveland that has pulled this off must be astounding to those who
once referred to the industrial city as "the Mistake on the Lake."
Mob violence, a bankrupt government and a river so polluted it
caught fire are all part of Cleveland's heritage. Even in recent
history, Cleveland has taken is knocks. It suffered the indignation

at having its beloved football team, the Browns, hijacked to Boston where it was renamed the Ravens, as if to add a poetic epitaph, "...nevermore."

But the New Cleveland is having the last laugh. The city, which celebrated its bicentennial in 1996, has succeeded in turning its image around, applying a fresh coat of paint to a weathered facade. It hasn't erased its scars, but wears them with character, like the lines in an old man's face. One of Cleveland's charms is that it is a city with a past.

Today, the Cleveland skyline is an eclectic mixture of new and old buildings and monuments against the backdrop of Lake Erie. The corporate headquarters of Keycorp, the tallest building between New York and Chicago, built in 1992, is just a short walk from the Terminal Tower, the largest building in the world outside of New York when it was built 60 years earlier. A new mall, the Galleria at Erieview on Ninth Street, proves that people will still shop downtown, a trend started a century before at The Arcade, the nation's first mall, which is still open on Euclid Avenue. The recently vacated headquarters of BP America, completed in 1985, looms over the city built with the money of oil barons.

The Cuyahoga River, once a rallying point for a budding environmental movement in the United States, is now a party place for fun-lovers drawn to all the new nightspots. And the Browns are back, too, in a brand new lakefront stadium not far from the new ballpark and arena where the Indians and Cavaliers play.

Joan Tiefel Photo

Cleveland skyline.

Cleveland's revival has added still more layers to the rich texture of one of America's most storied cities. With the addition of the Rock and Roll Hall of Fame and Museum, you might even say Cleveland's got a brand new bag.

Cleveland: Old and New

A young Yale graduate and attorney named Moses Cleaveland led the first survey party here in 1796 with orders to lay out a town and subdivide the Western Reserve into townships. It was miserable for the first survey crews who landed at the flats. Almost all of them contracted ague fever (malaria) or dysentery. For almost 30 years, settlers in isolated areas struggled to eke out a living, using Indian trails to lay out crude roads. As for Cleaveland, he stayed only a few months before returning to Connecticut. He never returned.

Cleveland (the spelling was inexplicably changed in 1831) was just one of many towns to spring up in this era. Fairport, Painesville, Mentor and Lorain were equal in size and stature. That changed with the opening of the Akron to Cleveland section of the Ohio and Erie Canal in 1827, creating outlets for agricultural products and other commerce. By the time the railroads came in the 1850s, Cleveland was already the dominant city west of Buffalo.

Shipping was the catalyst for Cleveland's growth. The giant bulk carriers brought back ore from the upper lakes to be fabri-

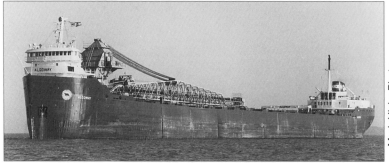

Shipping was the catalyst for Cleveland's growth.

cated into products in foundries fired by coal brought up the canal from the southern part of the state. But it was another buried treasure that would truly transform the city.

Oil was discovered in Pennsylvania and Cleveland became the refining center of the nation. Prosperity poured into the city where the Rockefellers made their fortune. Skyscrapers shot up in downtown and mansions lined Euclid Avenue. By the 1950s, Cleveland's population approached one million, making it the largest city in Ohio, one of the 10 largest cities in the nation and an economic powerhouse in the Midwest, rivaling even Chicago.

In recent years, the city has lost population, slipping to Ohio's No. 2 behind the capital, Columbus, and tumbling to No. 23 in the country. But this trend is not unique to Cleveland, which has worked hard to overcome its Rust Belt image. Today the staunchest critic of the city would have to be impressed with its new shine.

The cornerstone of The New Cleveland is the sparkling $324 million Gateway complex in the southern section of downtown. Gateway is home to the Indians' 43,300-seat Jacobs Field and the Cavaliers' 20,000-seat Gund Arena, which opened months apart in 1994. The opening of the stadium and two trips to the World Series in three years gave Clevelanders a rallying point and focused national attention on the shores of Lake Erie.

In the spring of 1997, the city broke ground for a $240 million, 72,000-seat football stadium on the lakefront site where the

Joan Tiefel Photo

***The new stadium for the
"new" Cleveland Browns.***

Brown's and the Indian's once shared cavernous Cleveland Stadium. The new stadium is home to the new Browns, an expansion
team that kept the name of the franchise that moved to Baltimore at
the end of the 1995 season.

Buoyed by these people-magnet venues, Cleveland has basked
in its newfound success. It has even taken to calling itself the
"New American City."

Music now pulsates from a 100-year-old power plant that used
to run the city's streetcars. Upscale eateries occupy warehouses in
what used to be a grimy industrial area. The Flats/Warehouse
District, centered around the Nautica Entertainment Complex on
the west side of the river, now sprawls along both banks, offering
everything from family dining to strip clubs and catering to all
manner of modern musical tastes. The Flats has come to symbolize
the very spirit of Cleveland, as if the city were literally dancing on
the grave of its tired old image. The Flats, like Cleveland itself,
ain't what it used to be.

On the other hand, one of the attractions of Playhouse Square
is that it is a lot like it used to be. The three elegantly restored
1920s movie houses — the State, the Ohio, and the Palace — now
house the Cleveland Ballet,
Ohio Ballet, Cleveland Opera
and Great Lakes Theater
Festival.

The Terminal Tower,
once a hub for rail passengers, is now a hub for shoppers at the Avenue at Tower
City Center. Boutiques,

*Cleveland's Terminal
Tower is a hub for
shoppers.*

Joan Tiefel Photo

eateries and movie theaters make up this underground mall that stretches all the way to Gateway. The Arcade, a restored glass-topped, Victorian shopping center, and the new glass-topped Galleria make up the city's central shopping area.

The 700-foot-tall Terminal Tower is the focal point of Public Square, which was designed by the New England founders as a place for the people to gather. The square has statues of Moses Cleaveland and Tom L. Johnson, mayor from 1901 to 1909, the Soldiers and Sailor's Monument and the Light of Friendship memorial.

A block away is the Mall, a rectangular park stretching to Lake Erie. City Hall, the public library and other local, state and federal government buildings line its perimeter. A scenic spot on the Mall is the War Memorial Fountain, quite possibly the most photographed spot in the city, with its large human figure reaching for the sky.

The West Side Market, just a few miles from downtown on West 25th Street, is a different kind of shopping experience. More than 100 vendors peddle fresh fruits, vegetables, meats, fish, poultry, cheeses, baked goods and ethnic foods here. The market is located in Ohio City, a community of European immigrants whose rivalry with Cleveland is perhaps best illustrated by the burning of the bridge that once connected the cities on opposite banks of the Cuyahoga. Ohio City became part of Cleveland in 1857, but maintains its own identity as one of the city's many ethnic neighborhoods.

Joan Tiefel Photo

More than 100 vendors peddle fresh produce, meats, fish, cheeses, baked goods and ethnic foods at the West Side Market.

They Built This City on Rock and Roll

Cleveland is where disc jockey Allan Freed coined the very phrase "rock 'n roll" and where Freed is memorialized alongside some of the world's pop culture icons in the Rock and Roll Hall of Fame and Museum. In this collection is everything from John Lennon's spectacles to Roy Orbison's shades, from The Supremes "butterfly gowns" to Michael Jackson's sequined glove; Elvis' black leather stage outfit to Jim Morrison's Cub Scout uniform. The 1968 acoustic Gibson Pete Townsend used to compose the rock opera "Tommy" is just one of 75 historic guitars on display, alongside one of The Who's broken tambourines.

Exhibits chart the history of rock since before its birth by recognizing early influences such as bluesman Elmore James and non-performers like producer Phil Spector who contributed to the evolution of the musical form. The inductees, from the Allman Brothers Band to Frank Zappa, are of course prominently featured. (An artist or group is not eligible for the Hall of Fame until 25 years after the release of its first recording.)

The Hall of Fame has existed on paper since Chuck Berry was inducted in 1986. Ten years later, the home of rock and roll opened at North Coast Harbor at Cleveland's Ninth Street Pier — a six-level "glass tent" designed by world famous architect I.M. Pei.

The Rock and Roll Hall of Fame and Museum.

University Circle

Long before there was a Rock and Roll museum, Cleveland was already a major arts and entertainment center. University Circle, five miles from downtown Cleveland in a one-square-mile block is the world's largest concentration of cultural, art, history and church institutions. This city-within-a-city, with wide boulevards and manicured landscapes, is home to Case Western University, the world famous Cleveland Clinic, numerous churches and more than 20 museums, galleries and theaters.

University Circle, which grew up around the now-combined Case and Western universities, has nine major museums and a total of 45 member institutions and 36 associate member institutions. Below is a sampling of what you will find here.

◆ The Cleveland Center for Contemporary Art showcases the works of national and international artists as well as those from the region.

◆ The Cleveland Botanical Garden is a non-profit educational institution on 10 acres featuring the Japanese Garden, Mary Ann Sears Swetland Rose Garden, Nona Whitney Evans Reading Garden, Western Reserve Herb Society Garden, and the Wildflower Garden. All are open to the public free of charge. There's also a horticultural library with more than 16,000 volumes.

University Circle.

Joan Tiefel Photo

The Cleveland Museum of Natural History.

◆ The African American Museum presents information on the African American experience through exhibits about the African continent, the civil rights movement, innovations of black scientists and inventors and achievements in sports and art.

◆ The collection of The Cleveland Museum of Art (CMA) includes nearly 40,000 works of art from ancient Egypt to the present.

◆ One of the Cleveland Museum of Natural History's newest attractions is PLANET e, which includes a simulated earthquake, outer space adventures and interactive video. It also houses the Wade Gallery, which has one of the finest collections of diamonds, opals and precious gemstones in the country, and exhibits featuring dinosaurs and other prehistoric creatures, ancient ancestors, changing modern-day cultures, animals and botany.

◆ The Dittrick Medical History Center and Museum houses historical materials that document the history of medicine. It has a rare book collection and the archives used to research a wide range of topics related to the history of medicine.

◆ Once a stagecoach stop on the old Buffalo-Cleveland-Detroit post road, Dunham Tavern Museum is the oldest building still standing on its original site in Cleveland. Located on the grounds is the Heritage Trail, a 900-foot path with life-size silhouettes depicting life in the Dunhams' days. The Klein Formal Garden exhibits flowers common to the mid-19th century.

◆ Among the other institutions are The Cleveland Children's Museum, the Cleveland Museum of Art, the Western Reserve

Historical Society and a museum of religious art. There are also eight performing arts and film centers, including Severance Hall, home of the Cleveland Symphony, four galleries and an outdoor sculpture tour.

More Museums

Other museums make serious fun of learning about science and technology:

◆ The Great Lakes Science Center, the $55 million next-door neighbor to the Rock and Roll Hall of Fame at North Coast Harbor, opened in 1996. It features more than 400 hands-on exhibits about the Great Lakes environment, technology and science, a "Polymer Funhouse" and an Omnimax theater that surrounds viewers with sights and sounds.

◆ The Steamship William G. Mather hauled iron ore on the Great Lakes for 60 years. Now, it is a floating museum run by the Great Lakes Historical Society at North Coast Harbor.

◆ The Visitor Center at the NASA Lewis Research Center, a leading power and propulsion facility, has displays that include a moon rock, an Apollo Skylab III command module, a space shuttle model and a replica of the solar system. Many of this aerospace museum's innovative exhibits are interactive. Tours are available.

Convention & Visitors Bureau of Grater Cleveland

The Visitor Center at the NASA Lewis Research Center has numerous displays.

Sports

Cleveland, Buffalo and Detroit make up a triumvirate of major league sports towns on the shores of Lake Erie. In Cleveland, sports fans and weekend warriors have their pick of major league baseball, football and men and women's basketball, plus minor league hockey and soccer and an international auto race.

◆ The Cleveland Indians American League baseball team plays at Jacob's Field.

◆ The Cleveland Cavaliers of the National Basketball Association, the Rockers of the Women's National Basketball Association, and the Lumberjacks International Hockey League team play at Gund Arena.

◆ The Crunch, of the NPSL Indoor Soccer league, plays at Cleveland State University's Convocation Center.

◆ Medic Drug Grand Prix of Cleveland is a three-day international auto racing event.

The Greater Cleveland area also has more than 300 private and public golf courses, horse racing at Northfield Park and Thistledown Racetrack, charter fishing boats on Lake Erie and several nearby ski resorts.

Louie Anderson Photo

The Cleveland Indians American League baseball team plays at Jacob's Field.

Cleveland Metroparks Zoo

The Cleveland Metroparks Zoo, seventh oldest zoo in the U.S., is home to The Rainforest, a two-story, two-acre indoor jungle that is one of the nation's most unique animal attractions. The Rainforest depicts hundreds of species of tropical plants and animals, from Bornean orangutans to Madagascar hissing cockroaches in simulated South American, Asian and African habitats — there's even a simulated tropical thunderstorm.

The zoo was founded in 1892 and has grown to include more than 3,300 animals plus educational exhibits and programs. It is set in park-like surroundings with rolling, wooded terrain, tall oaks, lush greenery and colorful flowers.

Other large exhibits include Birds of the World, with more than 300 species, and the primate, cat and aquatics building with red pandas, snow leopards, gorillas, chimps and 35 displays of salt and fresh water sea life. The Northern Trek Area features cold climate species such as polar bears, Siberian tigers and reindeer. There is also Monkey Island, Harbor Seals, Waterfowl Lake, the pachyderm building, a birds of prey exhibit and a public greenhouse.

Convention & Visitors Bureau of Grater Cleveland

The Cleveland Metroparks Zoo includes more than 3,300 animals, plus educational exhibits and programs.

Outdoor Recreation

Cleveland, with its urban image, is not likely the first place to spring to mind for outdoor recreation. Yet the area has the busiest state park in Ohio, a local Metropark district known as the "Emerald Necklace" and Ohio's only National Park.

Cleveland Lakefront State Park is made up of six units stretching 14 miles from Wildwood Park on Ohio 283 east of the city to Edgewater Park off Ohio Route 2 at the western edge of downtown. Many of the units, including Edgewater, were city parks, some established more than 100 years ago. Incorporated in the parks are yacht and boat clubs, public marinas, beaches, multipurpose trails and historical sites. It is the busiest Ohio state park, drawing 8 to 10 million people a year.

Cleveland Metroparks are referred to as the "Emerald Necklace" because the parks and parkways form a chain that dangles around the city. The Metropark District consists of more than 19,000 acres, mostly in Cuyahoga County, plus parkways along rivers and ravines, six golf courses, riding stables, nature centers and the Cleveland Metroparks Zoo. Huntington Reservation in Bay Village west of Cleveland is the only Metropark on Lake Erie. Located on U.S. Route 6, it has a beach as well as the Lake Erie Nature and Science Center, which doubles as a rehab center for injured and orphaned wildlife.

Cleveland Metroparks are referred to collectively as the "Emerald Necklace" because the parks and parkways form a chain that dangles around the city.

Joan Tiefel Photo

***Birds of prey are often spotted
in the Cleveland Metroparks.
This injured bird lives at
Huntington Reservation.***

Ohio & Erie Canal Reservation,
opened in 1998, is the newest of the
Metroparks. It stretches through the
villages of Cuyahoga Heights and
Valley View, following a portion of
the 309-mile canal from Cleveland to
Portsmouth. The reservation is part
of an 87-mile American Heritage Corridor created along the old
canal between Cleveland and Zoar, Ohio. Another of the Cleveland
Metroparks, Hinckley Reservation, is famous for the annual return
of the buzzards and the festival to welcome the homely birds
home.

On the list of the most visited national parks, monuments,
wilderness and recreation areas in the United States, number six is
a 33,000-acre scenic stretch of the Cuyahoga River Valley between
Cleveland and Akron called Cuyahoga Valley National Park.
Operated by the U.S. Forest Service, it is made up of river flood
plain, streams and creeks, forested valleys and upland plateaus that
appear today nearly as they did when Ohio was first settled.
Formerly a National Recreation Area, it was named a National
Park in 2000.

The area has a reconstructed portion of the Ohio and Erie
Canal Towpath, a multipurpose trail that runs the entire length of
the park. Along the way are educational exhibits about the canal
and its place in history.

The Boston Mills Ski Area, located in the park, is the largest
ski area in northeast Ohio. The full-service ski area offers a variety
of runs from expert to beginner. Located in the Lake Erie "snow
belt," Boston Mills Ski Area runs a complete schedule almost
every year.

Also located in the National Park is Hale Farm and Village where visitors learn about life as it was for 19th century farmers, and make use of hiking, bike and bridle trails and picnic areas. Several small towns and villages in the park have restaurants, antique shops, bed and breakfast inns, gift shops and bicycle rental shops. Rail service to the valley is available from downtown Cleveland. There are two visitor centers within the park: the Canal Visitor Center on the northwestern, or Cleveland, side of the area; and the Happy Days Visitor Center near Peninsula, Ohio. Both are open daily 8 a.m. to 5 p.m.

Lakewood to Lorain

CIRCLE TOUR: Follow Ohio 2 through Lakewood to Rocky River, then follow US Route 6 west through Avon Lake and Sheffield Lake to the city of Lorain.

One of the oldest of Cleveland's nearly 50 suburbs, Lakewood is a 5.6 square mile community of 60,000 people, tidy neighborhoods and tree-lined streets.

The Clifton Park neighborhood in the northern section of town, with its winding streets and stately homes built by Cleveland's captains of industry, is listed on the National Register of Historic Places. Also listed on the Register is the 1835 white colonial house built on an old Indian trail by Lakewood's first settler. The building is considered to be one of the best examples of New England architecture in the area.

The drive along U.S. Route 6 from Cleveland to Lorain takes in a parade of newer homes set on the bluff overlooking the lake.

Lorain

Lorain, the seat of the county of the same name, is set on the west side of the mouth of the Black River at the mid-point of Ohio's North Coast. It has 21 miles of Lake Erie shore, much of it set aside for parks, beaches, marinas and piers. Its lighthouse is a Lake Erie icon.

Lakeview Park, on Route 6, features a boardwalk, concessions, rose garden, gazebo, fountain, grassy picnic areas, volleyball courts and lawnbowling areas. Just east of Lakeview is the second largest Bascule bridge in the world, which is pulled open by counter balance weights to allow sailboats and river barges to pass. Elsewhere on the shore, colorful sailboards are an almost constant part of the scene. In 1994, Lorain hosted the National Windsurfing championships.

The 3.5-mile Bridgeway Trail offers hikers and bikers a scenic path that runs from Elyria to Lorain, overlooking cliffs and traversing two bridges across the Black River.

Lorain County's historic architecture is the backdrop for dining and shopping in style. The French Creek Antique District in Avon Lake, a city in the northeast corner of Lorain County, has dozens of antique shops in restored historic homes.

Festivals

Lorain County, you could say, is a festive place. The community hosts an International Festival, an Afro-American Festival, and a Spanish Festival; a Corn Festival and an Apple Festival; a Port Awareness Day, Lighthouse Celebration and model shipbuilders' competition, among other events throughout the year. Its more than

Roger Brownson Photo

Just east of Lakeview is the second largest Bascule bridge in the world, which is pulled open by counter balance weights.

50 festivals include some of the largest in Ohio. The Ohio Scottish Games, for example, brings crowds from throughout the country and Canada to Oberlin each summer.

The Road to Freedom

SIDE TRIP: Oberlin, which is not on the Circle Tour, is 12-miles south of Lorain on Ohio Route 58.

Slaves slept here. They slept well, too, safe for perhaps the first time from the tyranny that drove them north in the early to mid 1800s in pursuit of freedom on Lake Erie's shores.

Ohio's port cities from Ashtabula to Toledo were important links in the Underground Railroad, a 23-state network of brave strangers ready with food, shelter and protection for an estimated 50,000-60,000 runaway slaves. Once here, they could cross over to Canada, which outlawed slavery in 1833.

Of all the "depots" on the outlaw railroad along the Lake Erie shore, the most famous was Oberlin in Lorain County, a junction that could be called the Grand Central Station of the underground. The town of Oberlin and the college that bears its name were known as far away as Europe as a "hotbed of abolitionism." It was even accused of being the town that started the Civil War. The college's faculty and co-educational students were seen as subversive because of their convictions included the belief in a higher law than the ones that made harboring fugitive slaves a crime.

In 1844 an African Methodist Episcopal Clergyman said Oberlin was "the only place in the United States where a black man might get an inexpensive education and at the same time, be respected as a man." Those who promoted slavery, or at least the status quo, held the Oberlin Collegiate Institute responsible for the town's radical reputation and tried to have the college's charter repealed in 1842 by accusing the abolition movement of treason, no less. History would see it differently.

In 1858, Oberlin brought international attention to the abolitionist cause when townspeople, including freed slaves, stormed a hotel in nearby Wellington to free fugitive slave John Price from four slave catchers who came to take him back to Kentucky. The rescuers helped Price escape to Canada at their own peril; 37 of them were later indicted and 20 of them served time in jail.

One hundred and ten years after that brave demonstration of defiance, The Rev. Martin Luther King, Jr., delivered a speech in Oberlin entitled "Remaining Awake Through a Great Revolution." He had come to the right place. Through the years, Lorain County has remained awake, claiming among its people the first black elected official in the United States, the first black woman college graduate and the original George Harris of "Uncle Tom's Cabin," the historical novel by Ohioan Harriet Beecher Stow.

Harris is buried in Westwood Cemetery along with numerous former slaves, famous abolitionists and others referred to as Oberlin's "Faces of Change." The cemetery, on Morgan Street, is one of several sites on an African-American Heritage Tour. Another stop, he First Church at Main and Lorain streets, was built in 1842 and became the meeting site for the Oberlin Anti-Slavery Society. It was also site of the funeral for a four-year old fugitive slave child and the memorial service for John Copeland and Shields Green of Oberlin who were hanged for their participation in John Brown's raid on Harper's Ferry.

More Information

Cleveland Metroparks Zoo
3900 Wildlife Way
Cleveland, OH 44109
216-661-6500
www.clemetzoo.com

Convention & Visitors Bureau of Greater Cleveland
3100 Terminal Tower, 50 Public Square
Cleveland, OH 44113-2290
Visitor Information Hotline, 800-321-1004
www.travelcleveland.com

Lorain County Visitors Bureau
611 Broadway Avenue
Lorain, OH 44052-1803
800-334-1673
www.lcvb.org

Rock and Roll Hall of Fame and Museum
One Key Plaza
Cleveland, OH 44114
(East Ninth Street at Lake Erie)
888-764-ROCK
www.rockhall.com

University Circle Inc.
10831 Magnolia Drive
Cleveland, OH 44106
phone: 216 791-3900
www.universitycircle.org

Dan Feicht Photo

Thrill seekers ride wild at Cedar Point Amusement Park.

CIRCLE TOUR: The Circle Tour continues west on US Route 6 through Vermilion, Huron and Sandusky, then follows State Route 2 west to Port Clinton.

Chapter 8

Vacationland and the Islands

The mention of Lake Erie is more likely to evoke images of hulking power plants and monstrous cranes than quaint cottages and colorful sailboats bobbing on blue water. This perception of Erie painted an industrial gray is not undeserved. She does work for a living — perhaps harder than any other body of water on the continent. But hospitality is among the region's many trades. Places like Sandusky and Port Clinton, Ohio, popular launch points to the lake's only island chain, make serious business of having fun.

Ferries, not freighters, carry the most important cargo in Vacationland, the midsection of Ohio's north coast between Cleveland and Toledo. The area known as Vacationland for more than 100 years is a hub of summertime activity — an area where commerce is measured in tourists, not tons. The region begins in Vermilion and includes Sandusky and the Marblehead Peninsula on opposite sides of Sandusky Bay.

Along other stretches of the shore we look out or down at water bordered by bluffs, but here, land and water are not so clearly defined. Sand spits and rocky peninsulas stretch outward toward islands like the ruins of ancient bridges, while man-made

causeways span gaps in the ground and marshy edges blur the line
between what is wet and dry. Nowhere do you feel more a part of
the lake. Nowhere on the shore is there more access to the water. It
is everywhere.

Vermilion and the Firelands

If Vacationland were a theme park created by Disney itself,
the entrance would have to look something like Vermilion. This
picture postcard of a town has been compared to Cape Cod and
Venice for its New England-inspired houses and cottages built
along finger-like lagoons where boaters tie up at their back
porches.

Vermilion lies within what was once the Firelands, 500,000
acres of Connecticut's Western Reserve set aside for residents of
that state burned out of their homes by British raiders during the
Revolutionary War. These settlers arrived here in the first decade
of the 1800s and built communities in the image of their native
seaside villages. The town became a prosperous shipbuilding
center in the 1840s and 1850s, the period in which many of the
stately homes of successful mariners were built.

When its major industry was drawn like a magnet to Cleveland in the 1860s, Vermilion settled in to a more relaxing groove.
Today visitors to its main tourist attraction, the Inland Seas Maritime Museum, take pleasure in strolling the streets of its neat
neighborhoods and the shops of Harbourtown, the renovated
downtown that recaptures the mood of its golden age.

*Vermilion is a
boater's paradise
and a scenic start
to Vacationland.*

Roger Brownson Photo

Timbers from Commodore Perry's ship Niagara and many other treasures are housed in the Inland Seas Maritime Museum.

Inland Seas Maritime Museum

Timbers from Commodore Perry's ship Niagara, the lens from Lake Huron's Spectacle Reef Lighthouse and the entire pilot house of the 1905 Great Lakes steamer Canopus are housed in a lakeside estate guarded by a replica of the 1877 Vermilion lighthouse. The pilothouse is not actually in the museum, but a part of it, connected by a walkway to the former Wakefield Mansion that has been home to the Inland Seas Maritime Museum since 1953. Visitors can take the helm on the bridge of the Canopus and gaze beyond the imaginary bow out on the lake where perhaps they will see a modern day freighter carrying on the tradition.

Operated by the Great Lakes Historical Society, the museum is the oldest and most complete of its kind on the lakes. Extensive collections of maritime artifacts, charts, photos and model ships tell the stories of war ships, freighters and ferries and the men who sailed on them.

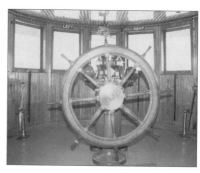

Lorain County Visitors Bureau

The Maritime Museum has a real pilothouse on display.

Woolly Bear Festival

What's a Woolly Bear? It's a fuzzy caterpillar and the festival that takes its name — the largest one-day festival in Ohio, held the last Sunday of September. The Festival of the Fish is held the third week in June.

Huron

The nearby city of Huron has a municipal boat basin with a park and amphitheater perfect for summer afternoon concerts. There are 125 seasonal and transient docks, a hotel, restaurants, a bathhouse, picnic areas and shopping nearby.

Huron has a Playhouse that is Ohio's oldest summer theater and a Historical & Cultural Center. It is also home to Sawmill Creek Resort, set on 300 wooded acres on the Lake Erie shore around a Fazio 18-hole golf course.

From Huron west lies Lake Erie's western basin, the shallowest, warmest and most biologically productive part of the lake. Averaging just 24 feet in depth, the "West End" has many characteristics that differ from the central and eastern basins, most notably its many reefs and islands.

Old Woman Creek/Sheldon Marsh

Three miles east of Huron on US 6 we reach the most southerly point of the Great Lakes and the Old Woman Creek National Estuarine Research Reserve. The 571-acre complex named for the creek that winds for 10 miles to Sandusky Bay is probably as close to a pristine natural area as you'll find along the Lake Erie shore. At the visitors center you will learn about the marshes, a swamp forest and the barrier beach at the mouth of the creek that separates the estuary from the lake. In 1980, Old Woman Creek was designated as a National Estuarine Research Reserve.

A few miles west of Old Woman Creek on U.S. 6 is Sheldon Marsh State Nature Preserve. One of the last remnants in Ohio of the forest-marsh-lake ecosystem, the 463-acre natural area also has

Old Woman Creek is a state nature preserve with a national designation because of its significance as an estuary.

some of the last wetlands and undeveloped shoreline on Sandusky Bay. The path through the preserve is what's left of the original road to Cedar Point amusement park. Even the old entrance gates remain.

Sandusky on the Bay

Sandusky Bay is enormous — one of the largest freshwater bays in the world. It is formed on the east by a sand spit off Sandusky called Cedar Point — home of the world famous amusement park of the same name — and on the west by the Marblehead Peninsula, marked by one of the Great Lakes' best known lighthouses.

The very name Sandusky comes from the Wyondot Indian word for water. Driving around the western shore of Cedar Point with its panoramic view of the bay, eating in a restaurant above a yacht club in Battery Park or traversing the bay causeway and bridge, you realize it could not have been named anything else.

Sandusky enjoys a national reputation as a summertime destination, mostly thanks to the amusement park. But Sandusky also has some of the most significant 19th Century and early 20th Century architecture in Ohio and a downtown that is set off by beautifully landscaped gardens.

Erie County hosts a series of events in September and October called Vineyard Days that include festivals, historic weekends, art shows, cruises and wine and cider events. Another series of events is held around the Christmas holiday.

Cedar Point

Cedar Point, in Sandusky, is like a city within a city. It has police and fire departments, shops and eateries, resort hotels, a campground and marina — even a dog-sitting service. In short, Cedar Point has everything any small town would have, with the notable addition of a dozen major roller coasters.

Cedar Point is one of the most popular tourist attractions on the Great Lakes and one of the oldest and best-known entertainment complexes in the United States, drawing more than 3 million guests each season. It began in 1870 as a bath house on a peninsula named for its cedar tree groves where guests rented bathing attire for 10 cents a day and danced in the Grand Pavilion.

The famous playground has hosted such celebrities of their time as sharpshooter Annie Oakley, composer John Philip Sousa, opera stars Enrico Caruso, Nellie Melba and Madame Schuman-Heink, and band leaders Woody Herman, Blue

Dan Feicht Photo

Cedar Point is one of the most popular tourist attractions on the Great Lakes and one of the best-known entertainment complexes in the United States.

Barron, Benny Goodman and Perry Como. Pioneer aviator Glenn H. Curtiss completed what was at the time a record 65-mile water crossing from Cleveland to Cedar Point. Famed Notre Dame athlete Knute Rockne once worked as a lifeguard here, where he and another football great, Gus Dorais, developed and perfected the forward pass. It was also here that Helen Keller made her famous speech to the Lion's International where she urged the club's members to be the "Knights of the Blind," as they still are today.

Cedar Point's greatest claim to fame, its thrilling rides, dates to 1892 when the first roller coaster, the Switchback Railroad, was built. In rapid succession, the park grew to include a hotel, midway, fun houses and ride after ride after ride. Today, park fans would be disappointed if each new season did not kick off with an inaugural ride on a taller, faster or more unique and thrilling ride than the one unveiled the year before. Once known as a quiet waterside retreat, Cedar Point today thrives on its ability to quench thrill seekers' zest for speed.

The amusement park has the largest collection of roller coasters in the world. It include sthe first triple-loop coaster, the Corkscrew; the first to break the 125-foot height barrier, Gemini; the world's tallest wooden coaster, Mean Streak, and the tallest, fastest inverted, ski-lift style coaster, the Raptor, which turns riders upside down six times. The coasters have gotten more adventurous since the days of the Switchback Railroad, which "thrilled" riders with a 25-foot drop at speeds of up to 10 mph.

The coasters are the main reason readers of "Inside Track," the only newspaper of the amusement and theme park industry, named Cedar Point best amusement park in the world in a 1994 poll. One of the park's roller coasters, the Magnum XL-200, was also voted number one coaster in the world in the international poll.

Parks, Natural Areas

◆ First planted in 1843, the gardens at Washington Park in Sandusky's downtown district still turn heads, especially the floral clock and blooming calendar. The statue of the Boy and the Boot is a local treasure.

◆ Battery Park on the bay is home to a marina, restaurant and lots of access for shoreline fishing, picnicking or leisurely strolls on the waterfront. From here, you can watch ferries headed for Kelleys and Pelee islands and the tallest humps of roller coasters rising from Cedar Point on the peninsula jutting into the bay. A new maritime history museum is located in the park. Surf's Up Aquatic Center, a city-owned wave action pool, is located next to the park.

◆ At Sandusky Harbor, off US Route 6 in downtown Sandusky, birders will find large rafts of waterfowl including migrating mergansers, egrets and night herons, black backed gulls in winter and a large colony of herring gulls. The 100-acre Pipe Creek Wildlife Area, on River Road off the Cedar Point Causeway, is home to Ohio's largest population of nesting common terns, a bird on the state's endangered species list. Bald eagles are also seen here.

◆ A short drive south from Sandusky on U.S. 6 is the Pickerel Creek Wildlife Area on the southern edge of Sandusky Bay. It is Ohio's premier wetland, with more than 1,100 acres of restored

Sandusky/Erie County Visitors & Convention Bureau

habitat for migrating water-fowl. There is also a bald eagle nest here. Adjacent to the wildlife area is Blue Heron Reserve, a Sandusky County Park.

The Merry-Go-Round Museum preserves a unique part of Sandusky's history.

Museums

◆ The Merry-Go-Round Museum, located in an historic old post office with a rotunda that looks like it was built for its current use, features a full carousel of painted ponies, an authentic carving shop, gift shop, tours and carving demonstrations. It is open year round at the corner of Jackson and West Washington streets.

◆ The Follett House Museum, 404 Wayne Street, a Victorian home, displays toys, clothing and furnishings of the period and artifacts of the Civil War. It is open April through December.

CIRCLE TOUR: Leaving Sandusky, the Circle Tour rejoins Ohio Route 2 and crosses Sandusky Bay. It exits on Ohio 163 (old Ohio 2) through Port Clinton, then returns to Ohio Route 2. A side trip marked with brown Lake Erie Circle Tour signs loops around the tip of the Marblehead Peninsula on Ohio 269 and Ohio 163.

On the Peninsula

Early inhabitants of the area followed the shore of Sandusky Bay 20 miles inland just to avoid a water crossing around the treacherous Marblehead Peninsula. The prominent point, which is shaped like a whale's tail, with Catawba going one direction and Danbury Township stretching the longer way out to the village of Marblehead, is vulnerable to wind and waves sweeping across the open lake.

In contrast to other parts of Vacationland, Catawba and Marblehead are almost non-commercial, void of chain stores, national hotel names and fast food restaurants. Bed and breakfast inns and private, mom-and-pop shops and restaurants are the norm here, lending to, or perhaps accounting for, the area's charm.

In Marblehead is a cluster of small gift shops, antique stores and art galleries centered on an old schoolhouse converted to shops. Neuman Boat Line and Kelleys Island Ferry Boat Line ferry people to Kelleys Island, which lies three miles off shore. The US Coast Guard Station Marblehead, located next to the ferry docks, is the busiest Coast Guard search and rescue station on the Great Lakes.

Catawba, one quickly concludes, is an affluent area. It is made up of private condominium communities on the lake side of the peninsula and marinas on the other side. Ohio Route 53 leads out to the tip, where the Miller Ferry waits to carry people and cars to Put-in-Bay. Gates and guard shacks leave no doubt where the casual visitor is welcome and where he is not.

Marblehead Lighthouse State Park

The Marblehead Lighthouse is the second oldest lighthouse on Lake Erie and the oldest in continuous service on all the Great Lakes. It is also one of Ohio's newest state parks. The lighthouse has been a guiding light to ships and boats off the rocky Ottawa County peninsula since 1822, a year after it was built. One of the most famous structures on all the Great Lakes, it has been featured on everything from a US Postage Stamp to special Ohio license plates.

The light has played an important role by warding off ships that could be driven into the rocky shore during nor'easters bol-

stered by a 200-mile stretch of open water that has been known to pile up waves as high as 12 feet. Even today the lighthouse flashes a

The Marblehead Lighthouse is the oldest in continuous service on all the Great Lakes.

guiding light every three seconds that can be seen up to seven miles away.

Located inconspicuously off a narrow drive behind St. Mary's Byzantine Catholic Church on Ohio 163 (E. Main St.), the light is an icon of Western Lake Erie and a popular tourist stop. Visitors not only see a working piece of history, they are treated to a sweeping view of Sandusky Bay. Visitors can see the lighthouse any day, but there are limited opportunities each summer to tour the inside of the building.

Other Parks

◆ Along Alexander Pike, a road that cuts through the LaFarge quarrying operation that occupies the center of the peninsula, an observant traveler will come across a small nature preserve named for the famous flower that grows there, the Lakeside Daisy. What might look at first glance like a barren wasteland – or the surface of the moon — is actually the home of a dozen rare plant species, the Lakeside Daisy being the rarest of all. The long-lived perennial grows in full sunlight in mid-May on the limestone bedrock unearthed during quarrying — truly a rare spectacle of nature.

◆ East Harbor State Park is a camper's park with 570 sites — more than any other Ohio state park. It is not unusual for every one of them to be full on summer weekends. East Harbor has a boat launch, nature center, a small but busy beach, trails for hiking, beautiful marshy areas and plenty of access to Lake Erie and

East Harbor State Park has 570 campsites.

backwaters for fishing. The park is located on Ohio 269 just a mile from Ohio 163, seven miles from Port Clinton.

◆ Quaint Catawba Island State Park offers a splendid view of the lake, with the city of Port Clinton on the horizon ahead and the Catawba bluff in the distance to the east, a notable exception to the mostly lake-level typography of Erie's western basin. There is possibly no better place to see a sunset over Lake Erie than from the rocky shoreline in the park, located off Ohio 53. It also has a boat ramp and fishing pier.

◆ Two boat accesses on the peninsula, both with large, open grassy spaces, could be called parks themselves. Dempsey-Sandusky Bay Access is located on County Road 135, five miles east of Ohio 269. Mazurik Access is on Lake Erie off Ohio 163. One end of the former Sandusky Bay Bridge, off Ohio 269, has also been preserved as a fishing access.

Lakeside

If there has not been a folk song written about Lakeside, there should be. This picturesque Victorian village is so inviting you can almost hear acoustic music wafting in the wind — or is that the strumming of strings drifting from the 3,000 seat Hoover Auditorium, which has hosted the likes of Pat Boone and Ray Charles. You are just as likely to hear a performance of the Lakeside Symphony Orchestra or the music of a visiting ballet company.

Lakeside is a private community — a chautauqua — bordered by a chain-link fence with a gate at the

A view of Lake Erie from Lakeside.

entrance where a small toll is collected in the summer. But don't take that to mean it is not inviting and hospitable, because it is very much both. Visitors are welcome and encouraged. It is just that the Lakeside Association keeps a standard to which its member-residents adhere. This is not a party place, but a gentle oasis with the characteristics one would expect of a Methodist summer retreat.

Lakeside was founded in 1873 as a religious summer camp and has been designated as a national historic district on the National Register of Historic Places. It remains a center for culture, religion, education and recreation. It is home of the National Shuffleboard Tournaments and boasts of having some of the finest clay tennis courts in the Midwest. It is also a pretty good spot to cast a line in the lake from the 700-foot pier or to spend an entire summer soaking up the good life on the sandy beach.

Accommodations are available at the Hotel Lakeside and the Fountain Inn, at the campground or by renting cottages. A brochure describes Lakeside as an ideal location for a "psychological retreat," a place where family and spirituality grow stronger.

Johnson's Island

Two hundred and six Georgia marble headstones mark the graves of Confederate prisoners who died on Johnson's Island during the Civil War. During its peak in January 1865, the 300-acre

Headstones mark the graves of Confederate prisoners on Johnson's Island.

island held 9,423 prisoners, including 26 Rebel generals. The cemetery, a few building foundations, one earthen fort and part of another are all that remain of the 15-acre prison.

The island is accessible by an automobile causeway with a $1 toll located at the end of Gaydos Drive, off Bayshore Road. A small wooden sign that is easy to miss is the only clue to the turn-off. Once over the causeway, the cemetery is straight ahead. Visitors are welcome there, but the rest of island is privately owned. There is an annual Memorial Day celebration with Civil War reenactors.

Area Attractions

◆ Mon Ami Restaurant and Historic Winery, built in the 1870s, offers tours and wine tasting. Located at 3845 Wine Cellar Road, Catawba.

◆ African Safari Wildlife Park, 267 Lightner Road, Port Clinton, is a drive-through zoo where visitors feed giraffes, zebras and a variety of exotic deer from their cars. There are camel and pony rides and daily pig races.

◆ Train-O-Rama, on Ohio Route 163, Port Clinton, is Ohio's largest multi-gauge train display.

African Safari Wildlife Park

African Safari Wildlife Park in Port Clinton.

Port Clinton: Walleye Capital of the World

Western Lake Erie is a fish factory known as the Walleye Capital of the World, a distinction the city of takes to heart. The community is so proud of its famous fish that at the stroke of midnight on New Year's Eve, it drops a giant walleye in the tradition of New York's famous sparkling ball.

On the north shore, walleye are harvested as a cash crop by a fleet of commercial fishermen who put the tasty "pickerel" on menus of restaurants around the lake and across North America. Here on the south shore, the commercial catch of walleye has been illegal since the early 1970s. Ohio reserves this resource instead for the throngs of sport fishermen who make up the multi-million-dollar fishery.

Port Clinton, at the mouth of the Portage River, is a fisherman's village at heart, but today the fishermen are more likely to be the kind to wear khaki shorts and golf shirts than hip boots and suspenders. Arrive in town in the summer just about dawn and you will find streams of fishermen headed to the docks after a hearty breakfast at one of several mom and pop diners. Marquees outside carry-outs and gas stations advertise bait for sale with succinct signs like "Shiners, Yes!"

At the foot of Madison Street is the Port Clinton Fish Co., where what remains of Ohio's beleaguered commercial fishing fleet come to trade their haul and sport fishermen come to turn coolers of yellow perch into tasty fillets for the freezer. "Headboats," so called be-

Lake Erie is the undisputed "Walleye Capital of the World."

Mark Hicks Photo

cause anglers pay a fee per head to board, leave the mouth of the river alongside the ferryboats bound for Put-in-Bay. At virtually every marina, private charter boats operate "six packs," taking groups of six for four- or eight-hour fishing excursions in pursuit of walleye in the spring and summer and yellow perch and small-mouth bass in the fall.

Port Clinton is as far west as settlement once went, as a forbidding swamp lay to the west. Today, the small city is the heart of Vacationland and the seat of Ottawa County, with its 107 miles of Lake Erie shore. The city has a duel personality: small, friendly community in winter surrounded by half-empty condominium complexes on the shoreline, and bustling party place in summer where tens of thousands of funseekers set sail for the islands and all those condos light up at night.

CIRCLE TOUR: The Lake Erie Islands in the U.S. are accessible by ferryboats from Sandusky, Port Clinton, Catawba and Marblehead and by airplane from the Sandusky and Port Clinton airports.

The Islands

From the air, they look like steppingstones across the sea between the U.S. and Canadian shores. From a boat, they appear as oases in a vast blue-green desert, promising refuge from one of Lake Erie's infamous storms or a place to put in for the night. There are more than 20 islands strewn across the western basin of Lake Erie. Discovered more than 300 years ago by French fur traders, they have played historic roles in war and lured generations to their peaceful shores.

Most of these islands are not depicted in brochures. Birds, and only birds, flock to West Sister, a sanctuary and Ohio's only designated federal Wilderness Area. Students study on Gibraltar and grapes grow on North Bass and Middle Bass while privately-owned Rattlesnake, once home to a famous club of the same name, keeps to itself. Mouse, Green, Ballast, Starve, Gull and Sugar

South Bass Island features Put-in-Bay and Perry's Monument.

Ohio Sea Grant

islands — all private — go mostly unnoticed, save for boaters and fishermen for whom they are like mile markers on a highway.

Put-in-Bay and Kelleys Island, with their Victorian charm, are the people places of the western Lake Erie islands — vacation destinations as different from each other as they are from the mainland. Pelee Island is their Canadian cousin (see chapter 2 "Ontario: Along the Lakeshore"). Throngs of tourists arrive at these islands daily by ferries, cabin cruisers, sailboats, even Jet Skis, to revel and relax in a carefree atmosphere as carefully cultivated over a century as a row of ripe Catawba grapes.

Put-in-Bay

There has been a song written about Put-in-Bay, and appropriately enough it is a rip-roaring crowd-pleaser — call it a drinking tune. Put-in-Bay, the island like the song, is a good time. The village that inhabits South Bass Island, and the name by which the island itself is best known, Put-in-Bay has been a popular resort since shortly after the Civil War. Here you will find attractions that range from wholesome family fun to adults-only entertainment — a place that boasts both the third tallest national monument in the U.S. and "the longest bar in the world."

Perry's Monument

Perry's Victory and International Peace Memorial is perhaps the most readily identifiable man-made landmark on the Great

Lakes. The 352-foot-tall Greek Doric column is made of Milford granite brought here from Massachusetts. It was built between 1912 and 1915 and paid for by nine states. The column is tapered from base to top and crowned with an 11-ton brass urn. The names of men killed or wounded in the Battle of Lake Erie are engraved in the walls of the rotunda made of Italian Marble, pink granite, Indiana limestone, Tennessee marble and brass. As a statement of international peace, the bodies of three American and three British soldiers are buried beneath the floor.

The Battle of Lake Erie on September 10, 1813, was a major turning point in the states' favor during the War of 1812. Commodore Oliver Hazard Perry's fleet of nine boats sailed from Presque Isle in Erie, Pennsylvania, to the Bass Islands in August to await the inevitable clash with British Captain Robert H. Barklay — a battle from which young Perry would emerge a national hero.

After several hours of fire, Perry and what remained of his crew left their burning ship, the Lawrence, and rowed to the unscathed Niagara, which had been laying back. By that afternoon, from the bridge of the Niagara, Perry had captured all six vessels of the British fleet. A few hours later at West Sister Island, 14 miles west of where the battle began, the brash navyman hastily scrawled a note on the back of a letter to his general: "We have met the enemy and they are ours, Two ships, two brigs, one schooner and one sloop."

Today, the Perry Monument stands not only as a memorial to the

Perry's Monument stands practically within casting range of superb smallmouth bass fishing.

Mark Hicks Photo

heroic battle that took place here, but to more than a century and a half of peace between the United States and Canada, who today share the longest unguarded international boundary in the world.

The monument's visitor center and a small museum are open Memorial Day through Labor Day.

Island Wines

It is not surprising that tourists started arriving on Put-in-Bay about the time the wine began to flow. Winemaking started on Kelleys Island, but in 1858, Joseph de Rivera St. Jurgo, who had recently purchased South Bass and five other islands, planted the first vines on Put-in-Bay. De Rivera had noticed how well wild grapes grew on the islands, thanks to a fortunate combination of limestone-rich soil and the moderating influence of Lake Erie on the climate, which extends the growing season.

In the next two decades the number of grape growers increased to 71 and together they harvested one million pounds of fruit. From 1858 to 1899, half of the islanders made their living from the wine industry and in the fall school children were given a two-week vacation to help their parents in the fields.

At one time, at least a dozen small wine presses operated on the island, along with two distilleries that made Catawba brandy. Today, just one winery remains: Heineman, on Put-in-Bay. The Meier's Wine Co. still grows grapes on Isle St. George, better known as North Bass Island.

Gustav Heineman came from Baden, Germany, in the 1880s to work in the vineyards on Put-in-Bay and build his own winery. In 1887, while digging a well under the present winery, he discovered a crystal-lined cavern — a giant geode about 30 feet across and encrusted with more than 50 tons of blue and white celestite crystal composed of strontium sulfate. Crystal Cave is now a tourist attraction along with the winery, both of which remain in the Heineman family. Heineman Vineyards is located at Mitchell Road at the corner of Catawba Avenue and West Shore Boulevard. Catawba (pink), Niagara (white) and Concord (red) are the main grapes grown on the islands.

Mark Hicks Photo

The Lonz Winery, now closed, is to become part of a new Ohio State Park.

The Lonz Winery produced wine on the southern tip of Middle Bass Island beginning in 1884. An accident there in the summer of 2000, when a terrace collapsed killing one man and injuring scores of others, was a tragic end to the winery, which was already slated to close at the end of the season. The winery and surrounding grounds are to become part of a new Ohio State Park. Opened during the Civil War as the Golden Eagle Winery, by 1875 the winery was the largest producer of wine in the country. Founder Peter Lonz reportedly drank 40 gallons of his wine a year — and lived to be 98 years old!

Put-in-Bay Attractions

South Bass Island has a variety of eating and drinking establishments, from the modern Beer Barrel Saloon (whose 160 bar stools and 56 beer taps account for the "longest bar in the world" claim) to the historic Round House Bar, Crescent Tavern and Crew's Nest, all established in the 1870s. Live music of all varieties entertains island visitors on summer weekends. Nearly a dozen hotels include one built in 1865 and a couple that are brand new. About a dozen bed and breakfast inns and numerous rental cabins and homes are also options for weekend or summer-long stays.

Put-in-Bay also has a large number of gift shops and specialty stores, a microbrewery and biplane and parasailing rides, among other attractions.

Historic Round House Bar.

The Beer Barrel Saloon boasts the "longest bar in the world."

Other Things to See and Do

◆ Perry's Cave, a 280-foot long cave 52 feet below ground covered with calcite deposits, is open for tours. It has an underground lake.

◆ Stonehenge is a stone house, barn and wine press cottage build about 1855 of local dolomite bedrock. (There are other historic homesteads on the island. A guidebook published by Ohio Sea Grant for sale at island stores describes many of them.)

◆ Lake Erie Islands Historical Society Museum has displays on the Battle of Lake Erie, the Ford Tri-Motor airplane that served the island for decades, island wildlife and model ships.

◆ Bay Players Summer Theatre, a professional theater company, presents family-oriented musicals and comedies in daily performances in July and August.

◆ Many of the island's historic icons, from the Commodore himself to the old Tin Goose airplane, are depicted in carvings that crown Kimberly's Carousel, whose organ music can be heard throughout downtown. One of the last wooden-horse carousels operating the US, it was built by Allen Herschell in 1917.

Parks & Natural Areas

South Bass Island State Park, on the southwest side of the island at the end of Catawba Avenue, is a quiet retreat. Thirty-two of its 134 campsites are on a cliff above the island's jagged shoreline. Four hexagonal "cabents" with tarp roofs are available for rent and there are a few transient boat docks. The park is a popular place for picnics or as a base for a weekend bicycling or fishing excursion. Victory Woods, located in the park, is the site of the former Hotel Victory, once billed as the world's largest summer resort hotel. It burned down in 1919, leaving only its great swimming pool, which islanders claim was the first co-ed bathing pool in the country.

◆ Oak Point State Park is a one-acre fishing access on the opposite side of Fishery Bay from Peach Point. An Aquatic Resource Center at Peach Point is an old state fish hatchery that now houses displays about aquatic life. Adjacent Terwilliger's Pond is a small natural area. Nearby Duff's Woods, former home of the Ohio State Music Camp, is a pleasant sugar maple forest.

◆ Lighthouse Woods, on the southernmost point of the island near the Miller Ferry docks, is loaded with hackberry and blue ash and a nice spot to view bedrock outcroppings. The South Bass Lighthouse, nearby, was built in 1895 by the US Coast Guard. It is now owned by Ohio State University.

◆ Put-in-Bay Beach, on the grounds of the 25-acre park surrounding the Perry Monument, is one of the few sand beaches on the island. It is open for public swimming.

◆ East Point is a scenic spot to view Ballast and Middle Bass Islands. West Shore Cove, on West Shore Road, is a scenic lookout on the sunset side of the island.

Times to Celebrate

Each of the spring and summer holidays, of course, are times for celebration on Put-in-Bay. Memorial Day and its Canadian equivalent, Victoria Day; the Fourth of July and Labor Day are particularly popular times.

South Bass Lighthouse was built in 1895.

There are also many other special events held on the island from spring through fall. The Blessing of the Fleet brings a parade of pleasure and working boats, including Coast Guard rescue vessels, to the island each April. The boats receive a blessing from clergymen as they pass the Jet Express dock near downtown.

Boats are also celebrated in June with the Mills Trophy sailing race from Toledo to Put-in-Bay. In August, the Inter-Lake Yachting Association sponsors junior, sail and powerboat regattas on different weekends in late July and early August. There is another regatta in October.

An annual Rib Burn-off competition is held each May. In June is Old Island Day/Founder's Day, held at de Rivera Park. In July, the Erie Islands Historical Society offers island home tours.

One of the largest events is the Historical Weekend in July, which often features tall ships, a Boy Scout Camporee and an 1812 military encampment.

The creative islanders also celebrate Christmas in July and New Years Eve in September. Oktoberfest and Halloween are also observed with typical island fanfare.

Gibraltar Island

Gibraltar Island, just a few hundred strokes from South Bass by rowboat across Put-in-Bay Harbor, is home to Ohio State University's Franz Theodore Stone Laboratory, the oldest freshwater field station in the United States and a refuge where students can immerse themselves in subjects like ichthyology.

Gibraltar Island is home to Ohio State University's Franz Theodore Stone Laboratory, the oldest fresh-water field station in the United States.

The lab is best known for its part in the clean up of Lake Erie starting in the 1970s. This is where the Center for Lake Erie Area Research (CLEAR), with its research vessel, Hydra, conducted its famous phosphorous tests. CLEAR, and the Ohio Sea Grant extension service, continue to operate the facility, where research today focuses on subjects like exotic species, mayflies, algae and fish populations.

The six-acre island was once the residence of railroad tycoon and Civil War financier Jay Cooke, whose home, Cooke's Castle, is listed as a National Historic Landmark.

Kelleys Island

If Put-in-Bay is Lake Erie's party girl, Kelleys Island is her shy sister. Kelleys easy-going manner, turn-of-the-century homes turned bed and breakfast inns and natural beauty create a pastoral setting suited for a second honeymoon or a weekend of bird watching. A national magazine once named it one of the best family vacation spots in the United States, while individual resorts have made it onto several other "best" lists over the years.

Kelleys is the largest island on the U.S. side of the lake — four square-miles with 18 miles of shoreline. It is located three and one-half miles from Marblehead, nine miles from Sandusky and eight miles from Put-in-Bay.

Restored Victorian mansions line the southern side of the island, where development has wisely been separated from the shore, leaving the sweeping views of the lake, with Marblehead and Port Clinton in the distance, for all to enjoy.

People come to Kelleys to soak up the scenery more than anything else. There are shops and restaurants and other tourist distractions, but Kelleys is best described as "someplace to be" rather than "something to do."

Irad and Datus Kelley, sons of a Connecticut judge who later moved to Cleveland, became familiar with the island on sailing excursions to Detroit. By 1836, the brothers had purchased all but 90 acres of the island from the Connecticut Land company for $4,475 and eventually bought the remainder. Four years later, the island was renamed Kelleys.

The island's main use in the 1800s was for quarrying and its limestone was considered to be the finest. Stone was sold by the cord — five and one-half tons — for building material. Everything from bridges to breakwalls to one of the locks at Saulte Ste. Marie was built with the stone. The Kelley family eventually consolidated the many independent quarrying operations into the Kelleys Island Lime and Transport Company in 1865 and the operation continued for 50 years. The quarry sat idle from the 1940s to the 1960s, when the operation resumed, operating until 1972 as Kellstone, Inc.

Parks & Natural History

The island geology is its most unique feature. Kelleys is famous for its glacial grooves, scars in the rock left by the mile-

Art Weber Photo

The rocky north shore of Kelleys Island is one of the most scenic locations on Lake Erie.

thick Wisconsonian Glacier when it retreated 12,000 years ago. The grooves are four and one-half miles long, 36-40 feet wide and 17 feet deep into the limestone bedrock. They constitute the longest and finest examples of glacial scoring in the Western Hemisphere. While most of the grooves were destroyed in the quarrying operation, a nearly 400-feet long by 25-feet wide and 15 feet deep sample is preserved on the island by the Ohio Historical Society and listed on the National Register of Natural Landmarks. It is the island's must-see natural attribute.

Also listed on the National Register is Inscription Rock, stone carvings on a rock attributed to prehistoric Indians and uncovered 100 years ago on the south shore of the island.

The East Quarry Trail, part of Kelleys Island State Park, rings one of the abandoned quarries and is gaining in popularity as a place to hike, mountain bike and hunt for fossils. Brochures are available at the state park headquarters. Scenic Horseshoe Lake lies at the east end of the quarry. In all, there are more than 5 miles of trails, including the 1.5-mile North Shore loop, which skirts the shoreline, revealing views of Pelee Island in the distance.

While quality bird watching and hunting have long been attributes of Kelleys Island, the island is just beginning to come into its own as a top-notch destination for nature lovers in the fast growing business of "ecotourism." Some island inns sponsor birding weekends, offering visitors a chance to sleep in a century-old home and wake with birds at first light.

Kelleys Island's glacial grooves are the longest and finest examples of glacial scoring in the Western Hemisphere.

Art Weber Photo

Of the 73 parks in Ohio's state park system, few rival the tent-flap view offered by the 129-site campground at Kelleys Island State Park. The park also has a sandy beach, picnic areas and two boat ramps. There is excellent smallmouth bass fishing from the shore, and two of the most recent additions to Ohio's state nature preserve system are located nearby.

Winemaking

It was Datus Kelley who brought a new industry to the island — wine making. He brought roots of Isabella and Concord grape vines with him from Rockport, Ohio, in 1842 and sold his first barrel of wine eight years later. Today, the Kelleys Island Wine Company keeps the tradition alive, although no wine is actually made on the island anymore. Visitors to the winery can, nonetheless, sample the latest vintage in the wine tasting room or country wine garden, dine in the restaurant, or relax or play on the vineyard grounds.

Attractions

◆ The Kelley Mansion, built during the Civil War as a wedding gift of Datus Kelley to his son, Addison, was purchased in 1933 by the Dominican Sisters of Adrian, Michigan. From 1945 to 1971 it was a girls' camp. Today, it is one of the many historic

homes and other buildings preserved on the island, many of which

The extremely rare Lakeside Daisy grows on Kelleys Island near the Glacial Grooves.

are now charming bed and breakfast inns, restaurants and gift shops in the downtown area. There is so much history here, in fact, that the entire island is listed on the National Register of Historic Places.

◆ The Lake Erie Toy Museum displays one of the most diverse toy collections in the Midwest — 1,000 toys made in the 1870s to the 1980s by nearly 140 manufacturers in 10 countries. It is located at Caddy Shack Square, which also features several shops and eating establishments.

Island Events

Kelleys Island finds many reasons to celebrate, starting with Winterfest in March and ending with a Halloween Parade. In-between is a welcome back party in April, Nest with the Birds weekend and Musicfest in May, Island Fest in July and Homecoming in August. In September? What else but a halfway to St. Patrick's Day Party at local taverns.

Getting There

An ever-changing variety of ferry services shuttle funseekers to Put-in-Bay and Kelleys Island from Sandusky, Catawba, Marblehead, Port Clinton and even from across the lake in Ontario. Tour vessels offer dinner cruises around the islands, bird watching excursions and other special trips. You can also travel by air — the

The Jet Express ferry boat leaves Put-in-Bay harbor.

only way to go in the winter — between the Port Clinton and Put-in-Bay airports.

Ferry Schedules

The Jet Express
Port Clinton
1-800-245-1JET
www.jet-express.com

Island Rocket
Sandusky
800-854-8121
www.islandrocket.com

Kelleys Island Ferry Boat Line
Marblehead
888-225-4325
www.kelleysislandferry.com

Miller Boat Line
Catawba
800-500-2421
www.millferry.com

Neuman's Kelleys Island Ferry
Marblehead
800-876-1907
www.neumanferry.com

CIRCLE TOUR: The Circle Tour rejoins Ohio Route 2 headed west to Toledo about 30 miles away. The tour takes a short detour from Ohio Route 2, inviting the traveler to stop in Oak Harbor, a charming village on the banks of the scenic Portage River, before returning to Ohio 2.

Camp Perry, on the north side of Ohio Route 2, is a National Guard base built in 1906. Since the first year it has been the site of the National Rifle and Pistol Matches, now held simultaneously with the National Rifle Association's national shooting competition. In both World Wars, thousands of doughboys and GIs went through this reception area for training before shipping out. During World War II, the Camp also served as a prison and held about 2,000 Italian and 2,500 German POWs. The camp is an open base and visitation is permitted. It has a beach, a clubhouse and a fishing pier. (During shooting practice, boaters have to be warned away from the range fallout area, which happens to include the reefs, site of the most productive fishing on the lake.) Next to Camp Perry was the Erie Army Depot, which served for 48 years (until 1967) as a depot with over 300 buildings and 1,800 civilian workers. Today, it is an industrial park.

About 10 miles east from Camp Perry is the 493-foot tall hourglass-shaped cooling tower of Davis-Besse, one of three nuclear power stations on Lake Erie.

More Information

Cedar Point
One Cedar Point Drive
Sandusky, OH 44870-5259
419-627-2350
www.cedarpoint.com

Kelleys Island Chamber of Commerce
419-746-2360
www.kelleysisland.com

Ottawa County Visitors Bureau
109 Madison Street
Port Clinton, OH 43452
800-441-1271
www.lake-erie.com

Put-in-Bay Chamber of Commerce
P.O. Box 250
Put-in-Bay, OH 43465
419-285-2832
www.put-in-bay.com

Sandusky/Erie County
Visitors and Convention Bureau
4424 Milan Road, Suite A
Sandusky, OH 44870
1-800-255-ERIE or 419-625-2984
Fax: 419-625-5009
www.buckeyenorth.com

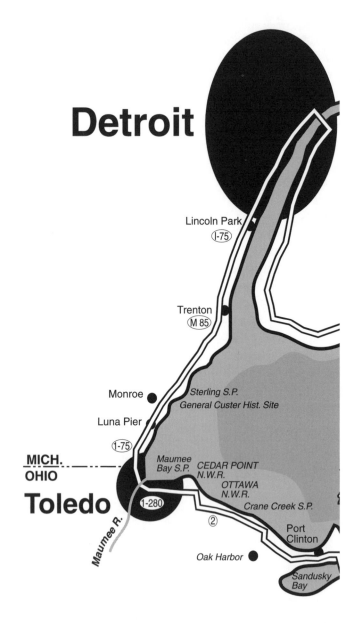

CIRCLE TOUR: Leaving Vacationland, the Circle Tour continues on State Route 2 to Toledo, about a 40-minute drive.

Section 4

The West End

The view from the beach at Maumee Bay State Park offers glimpses of Lake Erie's many personalities. To the left, the mouth of the Maumee River swallows freighters with bellies full of grain and coal. To the right, a tree-lined wildlife refuge juts into the water like a landing strip for weary birds looking for a place to set down. Pleasure crafts head for the horizon where the smokestacks of Michigan power plants stand as ghostly sentinels on the opposite shore.

In the West End, the hourglass shape of a nuclear power plant cooling tower rises from a marsh and a city skyline looms over fields of soybeans and corn. A torch from one of the oil refineries east of Toledo lights the sky over aging city-blocks in one direction and sprawling suburbs in the another. A busy highway comes to a sudden halt when a drawbridge opens for a ship leaving port.

Heading north from Toledo, this pattern of contrasting land-scapes continues — industry surrounded by agriculture, neighbor-hoods bordering natural areas. For a region whose topography varies from flat to flatter, it is not lacking in variety.

Toledo's metropolitan area stretches across the Michigan border until Detroit's influence takes over north of Monroe. The

A freighter on the Detroit River passes the city skyline.

two cities dominate the West End and swap auto parts and ball
players up and down I-75, but are distinctly separate places.
Toledoans routinely make the 50-mile trip to see a Tigers game
after work, or read the box scores in the Detroit newspapers with
their morning coffee, but the Glass City and the Motor City are
more like coworkers than neighbors. Each place has it's own
character, its own history, its own vibe.

***Rowers skim
the coffee-
colored
waters of the
Maumee
River in
downtown
Toledo.***

To the tourist, this region looks very different from other parts of the lakeshore. Contrary to the leisurely pace of the perpetual weekend that Vacationland seems to enjoy, the West End has to go to work in the morning. But bigger cities bring their own rewards and the proximity of Toledo and Detroit opens countless opportunities for the tourist to explore.

Around and between the cities you will find natural wonders that might even take you by surprise, beginning with The Marshlands.

Immature bald eagles have become more and
more common sights in the Lake Erie marshes.

Chapter 9

The Marshlands

O-ka-LEEEE! The song of a red-winged blackbird rises above the clamor of honks, chirps and muffled splashes that make up the music of the marsh. It's Mothers Day, but Mother Nature doesn't get to sleep in. The warblers are arriving, streams of them, and before the week is over up to 60 additional species will mingle with the local population until there are more birds here than almost anywhere else in the United States.

Not far behind the birds are the birders. You can spot the serious ones by the guidebooks sticking out of their fanny packs and the binoculars strung around their red necks. They set out on the boardwalk at Crane Creek State Park determined to add checkmarks next to the names of dozens of warblers on their life lists. Birders flock to The Marshlands for two obvious reasons: the number and variety of species, which increases their odds of seeing something they have never seen before, and the incomparable access to the birds' habitat afforded by the state and federal parks and preserves along the Western Lake Erie shore. It is birding bliss.

What even some of these wildlife aficionados may not know is that this region is the remaining piece of a once forsaken wilder-

*Birders flock
to the marshes
of southwest
Lake Erie.*

ness whose significance was not appreciated until most of it was
gone. Coastal wetlands are among the most productive places on
the planet, natural barriers between land and lake and vital links
between them. These habitats give life and sanctuary to a diverse
community that includes half the endangered species in Ohio.

The marshes of southwestern Lake Erie (what we refer to here
as The Marshlands) once stretched over 300,000-acres from Port
Clinton to Toledo, while a dark, forbidding woods continued south
and west along the Maumee River plain. It was known as the Great
Black Swamp. After 200 years of clearing and draining the land,
just 30,000 acres — a mere 10 percent — survives. State and
federal agencies and a few duck hunting clubs preserve remnants
of a complex ecosystem made up of open ponds, sandy beaches,
tall grasses and dense woods. Considering their location between
the major metropolitan areas of Cleveland, Toledo, and Detroit, it
is a miracle even this much is left. The U.S. Department of Geological Survey doesn't mince words when it describes the largest
of these preserves, the Ottawa National Wildlife Refuge, as "truly a
wildlife oasis in the midst of an urban biological desert." Suffice it
to say this is precious ground.

Wetlands — the broader term for marshes and swamps — are
important because they store the seeds of a wide range of plant
species, preserving genetic diversity that the world is losing on a
daily basis. They also function as the kidneys of the earth, filtering
the water before it enters the ground. Along the coasts, they absorb

Adult bald eagles are frequently sighted in the marshes of southwestern Lake Erie.

the energy of the waves that pound the shore, sparing the firmer ground from erosion.

These wetlands have added significance because of their location at the intersection of the Mississippi and Atlantic flyways — two important flight paths for migratory waterfowl. Hundreds of thousands of birds rely on the marshes for valuable resting, feeding and wintering habitat. For example, up to 70 per cent of the total black duck population in the Mississippi Flyway is concentrated here during fall migration. Migrating songbirds and raptors likewise use the marshes as stopovers in spring and fall during their long commute over or around Lake Erie, an obstacle the birds avoid because of its breadth and the lack of warm air columns, or thermals, they need to maintain altitude.

The marshes of southwestern Lake Erie are what remain of 300,000 acres that once stretched from Vermilion, Ohio to the mouth of the Detroit River.

Metroparks of the Toledo Area

What remains of The Marshlands is a living, breathing piece of our natural heritage, free and open to explore. If you like to watch wildlife, from red-tailed hawks to white-tailed deer, you will not find a better place. And after a long day in the wild, you can bask on the beach or lounge by the pool in the tame surroundings of a state park resort.

Magee Marsh Wildlife Area & Crane Creek State Park

The drive through Magee Marsh Wildlife Area from State Route 2 to the barrier beach known as Crane Creek State Park passes an incredible array of wildlife right outside the car window. The display is akin to a drive-through wildlife safari park only without the fence. This place is for real.

On the left, a deer pauses on the bank of the creek that separates the road from one of the marsh units. Dozens of goofy looking coots mill about in the water. Giant Canada geese stop traffic as they coax fuzzy brown and yellow goslings across the road, a comical scene that reminds the waiting motorists of an aggravated mother scolding inattentive children in the grocery store. The scene changes with the season, the day, and the hour.

Magee Marsh, part of what was once a 4,000-acre hunting club, is managed by the Ohio Department of Natural Resources, Division of Wildlife, which purchased the property in 1951. It is many things: hunting area, wildlife refuge, experiment station,

A project at the Magee Marsh State Wildlife Area, and other locations, has reintroduced Trumpeter swans, the largest waterfowl in North America, to the marshes of Lake Erie.

Crane Creek State Park is a beautiful beach shaded by tall trees.

state park, and nature education center. It is often referred to as the best birding site in Ohio and ranks among the best in the country. The marsh's 2,600 acres are managed for waterfowl using pumps to manipulate water levels in 27 miles of waterways to maximize vegetation the birds rely for food and shelter.

More than 300 bird species have been seen on the wildlife area. It is common at the right time of year to observe whistling swans, Canada geese, a variety of ducks, great blue herons, great egrets and even trumpeter swans, largest of all North American waterfowl. The Bird Trail, a 0.8-mile raised boardwalk near the beach, offers a rare opportunity to explore this fragile habitat and the best way to observe the wide variety of warblers, reptiles, amphibians, and small mammals that call the refuge home.

The Crane Creek Wildlife Experiment Station, established in 1956, administers statewide waterfowl, wetlands, and fur-bearing animal research and management projects. Research conducted here has involved rare plants, bald eagles, coyotes and, of course, waterfowl. As a result of the work on the marsh by state biologists, the US Fish and Wildlife Service once commended Ohio for "the most successful goose production project in the nation." The number of goslings raised here, 7,000-9,000 annually, is un-matched by any time in Ohio's recorded history.

The Bald Eagle Restoration Project began at Magee in 1979 when there were just four of the great birds left in the state. Today, more than four dozen eagles soar the Buckeye skies, with the greatest concentration of them found in the refuges along the

Magee Marsh is the center of Ohio's bald eagle restoration project. Young birds are banded and placed back in their nests as part of the program.

western basin of Lake Erie. Trumpeter swans are a more recent success story. Nearly a century after the last of the swans were hunted out of the marshes, several of the big birds were released here in 1996. State wildlife biologists collected eggs from nests in Alaska, incubated them at the Cleveland Metroparks Zoo, and reared them at a southeastern Ohio sanctuary called The Wilds before releasing them at Magee and other locations around the state.

The Sportsman's Migratory Bird Center is home base for the experiment station, as well as an education center where visitors can learn about the marsh habitat. The center has a large collection of mounted ducks, geese, and other birds and mammals typical of the marsh. A short trail, butterfly garden and viewing tower are located nearby.

A one-mile stretch of Lake Erie beach called Crane Creek State Park is located inside the wildlife area. It is a popular sunning, swimming and picnic area. Unlike other, wide-open beaches found in the area, Crane Creek has the added feature of tall shade trees. A Waterfowlers Festival is held at Crane Creek in late September and includes retriever trails, decoy and calling contests and vendors.

Ottawa National Wildlife Refuge

Exit Magee Marsh, turn right onto State Rt. 2 and right again at the next drive. You are now in the Ottawa National Wildlife

Refuge, at least the largest part of it. These 4,683 acres were set aside in 1961 under the authority of the Migratory Bird Conservation Act to preserve the dwindling Lake Erie marshes and to manage habitat for wildlife.

Ottawa is really an 8,316-acre complex of units that includes the 2,445-acre Cedar Point Wildlife Refuge on Maumee Bay and the 591-acre Navarre Marsh, which surrounds the cooling tower of the Davis-Besse Nuclear Power Station to the east. West Sister Island, which can be seen in the distance from the Crane Creek beach, is also part of the complex. The small island was designated as Ohio's only national wilderness area in 1938, and is a refuge for birds such as egrets. With the exception of the main unit, all of these areas are closed to the public except by permit.

The main unit on Route 2 has a small information center located inside the refuge office and restrooms near the parking lot, but otherwise offers little in the way of creature comforts for visitors. There are nine miles of trails in four loops, mostly along dike tops, and a viewing platform overlooking the marsh.

The opportunity to see bald eagles is reason enough to come to Ottawa. The refuge is noted for its nesting eagles, which are frequently seen soaring over the marsh or following the shoreline. The nest sites themselves are closed to the public and strictly protected.

*The marshes of western Lake
Erie teem with waterfowl.*

The refuge, like Magee, is managed for the birds, with water levels manipulated by dikes, ditches and pumps. Managed wetland units are drained in the spring and flooded in the fall to provide food and habitat for migrating waterfowl. Nearby farmers cooperate in the waterfowl management program by planting corn, sorghum and buckwheat that provide food and cover for the estimated 60,000 ducks of a dozen or more species and 25,000 geese that stop hear each year.

Metzger Marsh Wildlife Area

West of Ottawa NWR on State Route 2, just across the Lucas County border, is another state wildlife area called Metzger Marsh, a fishing and hunting access that is also popular with birders. A federal-state-private project is under way here to restore a wetland that had become totally exposed to the lake. In one of the largest projects of its kind in the nation, a 7,700-foot lakefront dike was built to separate the marsh from the lake and reclaim 908 acres of one of the last unprotected coastal wetlands on southwest Lake Erie. The conservation organization Ducks Unlimited is one of the sponsors of the project.

Metzger Marsh has a fishing pier that is especially busy in fall when yellow perch are biting. The access is also a popular destination for duck hunters and ice fishermen.

Waterfowl hunters appreciate the rich marshes of southwestern Lake Erie.

Deer are nearly always present at Maumee Bay State Park.

Maumee Bay State Park

Circle Tour: Maumee Bay State Park on Cedar Point Road is a short detour from the marked route. The park is accessible from State Route 2 by turning north onto Norden Road or North Curtice Road, either of which leads directly into the park.

Indoors mimics outdoors at the Milton Trautman Nature Center, where the sounds of frogs moaning and birds singing could be for real, or a recording in one of the colorful, life-like displays that bring the wonders of the marsh to life. The center is a good place to get your bearings before venturing out on the 2.5-mile boardwalk trail that loops through a wet-woods, over a pond, into a large field of reeds, and out to an observation tower overlooking the lake. The boardwalk is the longest in Ohio and an excellent place to watch wildlife, from snakes to deer, or Monarch butterflies, which are raised, tagged and released here.

Think of the Trautman Center as the wild side of Maumee Bay State Park, which has a much softer side as well. Amenities like a 120-room full-service lodge and 18-hole golf course make it one of the most popular of Ohio's eight state-park resorts.

Maumee Bay is a nearby getaway from Toledo, which is so close that the tallest buildings on the downtown skyline are visible from the beach across the flat landscape. Up to 15,000 people a day come here during the summer peak to row boats, sun them-

Boardwalks located at a number of marshes provide excellent access to view wildlife.

selves on the white sand that rings a 70-acre inland lake, or picnic on the mile-long Lake Erie beach. Others make a weekend of it at the Quilter Lodge, where they are pampered by all the niceties of a resort, like a restaurant, ballroom, indoor and outdoor pools, a health club, and a lounge. For a cozier retreat, there are also 24 family vacation cottages lined up on the edge of the links-style golf course, with its out-of-character rolling terrain built to resemble the courses of England or Scotland. For those who prefer to "rough it," there is a 256-site, full-service family campground on the opposite end of the park.

Other features of Maumee Bay include bicycle and walking trails traversing the entire park, a transient marina, watercraft rentals, a 3,000-seat amphitheater with hillside seating, and a winter recreation area with a sledding hill.

The Lake Erie Center, a research and education complex operated by the University of Toledo, is located in the northwest corner of the park and is accessible by Bayshore Road. Mallard Club Marsh is a state wildlife area that stretches from the eastern edge of the park to the Little Cedar Point National Wildlife Refuge along Maumee Bay.

Pearson Metropark

A local park is worth a stop before leaving the wilds behind for the big cities that rim the rest of Lake Erie's West End. Pearson Metropark, on State Route 2 in the city of Oregon, is a remnant of

Metroparks of the Toledo Area

Spring beauties ring the base of a cottonwood tree at Pearson Metropark, one of the last remnants of the Great Black Swamp.

the Great Black Swamp, a once impassible barrier to travel fraught with disease and heartache for settlers headed west in the early 1800s. The region was so dense with hardwood trees that from a distance it looked like a black wall. Army soldiers of the time described it as the most "forsaken, desolate and inhospitable wilderness" in America. It is also the reason that development of this region lagged behind the rest of the state by about 100 years.

Pearson Metropark today is a much friendlier place, with playgrounds, picnic shelters, and peddleboats on a scenic little pond that was hand-dug by workers of the Works Progress Administration during the Great Depression. Information panels describing the hardships of crossing the great swamp are located at the Packer-Hammersmith Center, where a Window on Wildlife looks onto a wildlife feeding station that attracts a large variety of birds. Though lesser known than the larger refuges on the lakeshore, Pearson is an excellent birding spot.

One of nine parks and preserves operated by the Metroparks of the Toledo Area, Pearson has an interesting history. It exists today because of the efforts of the citizens of the area and a crusading reporter for the Toledo Blade, George Pearson, who thought the woods should be preserved. The park district and a citizens group, Friends of Pearson Metropark, hold programs at the park throughout the year, including a Black Swamp Festival in the fall.

Marsh Wildlife

The Lake Erie marshes are home to around 300 species of birds, ranging from the tiniest finches to the largest swans. Over 250 species are considered regular visitors. It is possible in the spring to observe as many as 100 different species in a single day. In the summer, look for swallows, ducks, geese, coots and egrets. In the winter you might spot a short-eared owl hunting over the open marshes. Here are some other things you are likely to see.

◆ Dramatic flights of migrating warblers. Warblers are a family of birds known for their distinctive markings and bright colors in the spring. They have duller plumage in the fall, when even experienced birders may have trouble identifying them. They are often generically referred to as songbirds, although they don't necessarily have the best singing voices. The wooded areas of Magee Marsh, Maumee Bay and Pearson are the best places to see warblers, especially in spring when the population grows tremendously with the influx of migrating flocks. News travels quickly on the birding grapevine when a rare visitor is spotted, such as the Kirtland's warbler, a tiny bluish-gray songbird with a yellow breast and black streaks on its back.

◆ Waterfowl by the thousands. Canada geese and a variety of ducks are what you expect to find in a marsh. Because western Lake Erie is at the crossroads of two major "flyways," or air routes, for migrating waterfowl, they attract an incredible number of these water-loving birds, particularly in fall. The mallard is the

Red-tailed hawks are commonly seen throughout the region, often hunting fields.

Deer sightings are frequent in the marshlands of western Lake Erie.

dominant duck, but you will also see black ducks, widgeons, pintails, wood ducks, canvasbacks, redheads and the duck-like American coot (AKA the "mudhen"), among others. Tundra, whistling and trumpeter swans are the largest waterfowl that frequent the marshes.

◆ Wading birds and shorebirds. These graceful, long-legged beauties are another icon of the marsh. Great blue herons, great egrets, black-crowned night herons, green herons, bitterns, and killdeers are all common sights.

◆ Bald eagles and other raptors. Bald eagles nest in the marshes from February until the young fledge in July. Eagles can be observed throughout the year, but the numbers are greatest in the fall when eaglets fledged from northern territories migrate south. Note that immature bald eagles do not have the distinctive white head. Turkey vultures, red-tailed hawks, broad-winged hawks, and American kestrels are other commonly seen raptors. Even snowy owls visit from time to time.

◆ Reptiles and amphibians. Some of the species you might see include fox snakes, northern water snakes, Blanding's and painted turtles, green frogs, bullfrogs, and spotted salamanders.

◆ Mammals. Raccoons, muskrats, mink, fox, skunks, opossum, cotton-tail rabbits, groundhogs and deer are common sights.

◆ Insects. Dragonflies and damselflies in the summer. (Mosquitoes, too. This is the swamp!)

International Migratory Bird Day

The second Saturday in May — prime time for the spring migration of neotropical birds like warblers — is celebrated as International Migratory Bird Day at Magee Mash, Crane Creek, Ottawa and Maumee Bay. Bird banding demonstrations, wagon rides, nature walks and other programs welcome the return of the birds to Lake Erie's south shore. Some areas of Ottawa that are normally closed to vehicular traffic are open for drive-through tours.

More Information

Black Swamp Bird Observatory
P.O. Box 228
Oak Harbor, OH 43449
419-898-4070
www.bsbobird.org

Crane Creek State Park
(Contact Maumee Bay State Park or
Magee Marsh Wildlife Area)

Magee Marsh Wildlife Area
13229 West State Route 2
Oak Harbor, OH 43449
419-898-0960
www.dnr.state.oh.us/odnr/wildlife

Maumee Bay State Park
1400 Park Rd. #1
Oregon, OH 43618
419-836-7758
Quilter Lodge: 419-836-1466

Lodge/cabin reservations: 800-282-7275
www.dnr.state.oh.us/odnr/parks

Metroparks of the Toledo Area
5100 W. Central Ave.
Toledo, OH 43615
419-535-3050
www.metroparkstoledo.com

Ottawa National Wildlife Refuge
14000 West State Route 2
Oak Harbor, OH 43448
419-898-0014
www.fws.gov

Fireworks burst over the freighter Willis B. Boyer, now a maritime museum, during a Fourth of July celebration in Toledo.

CIRCLE TOUR: The Circle Tour continues west on Ohio State Route 2, through the city of Oregon, then north on I-280 through Toledo. I-475 splits off to the west into Toledo, while the Circle Tour continues north on I-75 toward Detroit.

Chapter 10

Toledo & Southeast Michigan

The best seat in Toledo is a park bench at International Park, a comfortable perch from which you can survey the city skyline or watch a freighter shuttle grain down the Maumee River through the parted span of the Martin Luther King, Jr. Bridge and out to the bay. You can spy members of a rowing club as they skim the coffee-colored waters of the largest river flowing into the Great Lakes, or a sea of people funneling into Promenade Park on the opposite bank for a free Friday afternoon concert.

International Park takes in more than a mile of riverfront stretching from the King Bridge to the taller, blue Anthony Wayne Bridge and includes a riverfront entertainment complex called The Docks with five full-service restaurants. Adjacent to The Docks is The Beach, a sand volleyball complex where large tournaments are held against the backdrop of the city skyline.

The park is not only a scenic spot to watch the world go by or relax with a beer on the patio of the Navy Bistro, it is symbolic of the city itself as a thread in the international web of commerce. Flagpoles posted along the crescent boat basin fly the colors of the nations linked by this busy seaport. The big boats tied up in the

The best seat in Toledo just might be a park bench at International Park.

park on winter layover are reminiscent of the property's previous life as a port facility where a honeycomb of railroad tracks, coal cars, cranes and buckets fed the hulls of freighters destined for ports around the Great Lakes. Even today, the drone of a ship's horn in the harbor is as common here on a summer night as the rumble of a train racing coal to the docks.

A living example of this shipping tradition, the 617 foot SS Willis B. Boyer, moored near the Anthony Wayne Bridge, lets visitors experience for themselves what it is like to stroll the deck of a freighter and peer through a porthole in the captain's well-appointed quarters. The museum hosts school children, tourists, corporate parties and social events.

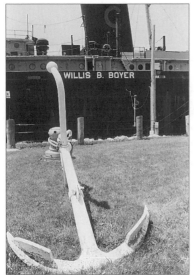

The Willis B. Boyer was once the Queen of the Great Lakes. Now the freighter is a living museum permanently moored at Toledo's International Park.

The green glass tower that dominates the downtown skyline across the river is the world headquarters of Owens Illinois, the Fortune 500 container manufacturer. Follow the Maumee upstream with your eyes to the campus-like headquarters of another Owens, building materials giant Owens Corning, jutting into the river. Edward Drummond Libbey moved his glassworks company here in 1888 from New England, but it was a Libbey employee, Michael J. Owens, who reinvented an industry with the development of an automated bottle-making machine in 1901. Two other long-time Toledo industries trace their roots to these glass pioneers: tableware-maker Libbey Glass, and the auto glass firm Libbey-Owens-Ford, now Pilkington. Toledo is perhaps more famous today for assembling Jeeps, which are made here in both the oldest and newest auto plants in the nation, but it is still known as the Glass City and still makes everything from wineglasses to windshields.

River City

The Maumee cuts through the flatlands of the Heartland from Fort Wayne, Indiana, to the Port of Toledo on Maumee Bay — "fort to port," as they say. (The name Maumee is said to be a mispronunciation by French settlers of the Indian word for the stream, "Miami.") The river is the most prominent feature of this city, which was formed on the edge of the Black Swamp in 1836. A mosaic of a frog still adorns the entrance to the Lucas County Courthouse as a reminder of the city's old nickname, "Frogtown."

Promenade Park along the waterfront opposite International Park is the site of free public concerts in the summer. Live music, food and beer draw the Friday after-work crowd and boats tie up along the river, adding to the festive atmosphere. Art and music festivals are held here on Memorial Day, Fourth of July weekends and Labor Day.

Plans for the redevelopment of Toledo's riverfront on both sides of the Maumee are so numerous and evolving it is difficult to predict what the waterfront will look like even a few years from now. A federal government building on the downtown side was torn down and a former steam plant in Promenade Park has been

Promenade Park is Toledo's festival place on the river.

earmarked for shops and other uses. The most ambitious plans, however, call for a new entertainment strip on the opposite side of the river called the Marina District. It would be located downriver from The Docks complex and include a new arena, 10 restaurants, movie theaters, hotels, offices, condominiums and boat slips.

The largest development in the works is a cable-stay bridge to replace the Craig Memorial Bridge, the drawbridge that now carries I-280 across the river. The Craig — one of two drawbridges over the Maumee — will remain for local traffic while the new bridge will become a new icon of the Toledo skyline.

Wading for Walleyes

Another stretch of the Maumee is the center of attention for a different reason in the spring. The Maumee has one of the world's largest river-spawning populations of walleye and the largest on the Great Lakes. Between late March and mid-April the river swells from snowmelt and rain, opening the way for a half-million of the popular game fish to swim upstream to spread their eggs among the protective gravel and cobblestone just below Fallen Timbers Rapids. Each female broadcasts hundreds of thousands of eggs, which contributing substantially to the walleye population.

Not surprisingly, this section of the river, which is flanked by the cities of Maumee and Perrysburg, is where you will find thousands of fishermen wading and waiting, rods clenched in their hands, landing nets tucked in the backs of their rubber waders. The

When walleye swim up the Maumee River for the spring spawn, fishermen wade after them, a phenomenon unmatched on the Great Lakes.

"spring run," as it is called, is a fishing phenomenon unequalled on the Great Lakes. Fishermen, by the way, take about 10 percent of the fish in a good year — a tiny fraction of the estimated 60 million walleye in Lake Erie, the Walleye Capital of the World.

Toledo Zoo

Toledo Zoological Gardens is the city's most popular attraction. It has more than 2,000 exotic animals of 400 species, including giraffes, leopards, rhinos and elephants. The African Savanna exhibit has the world's only "hippoquarium." There is a petting zoo, Museum of Science, a hands-on Diversity of Life display, one

The Toledo ZOO has more than 2,000 exotic animals of 400 species.

of the largest fresh and saltwater aquariums in the country, and botanical gardens.

Several new exhibits opened in 1999 and 2000 to coincide with the Zoo's 100th anniversary. At Arctic Encounter, visitors can see polar bears playing in frigid water. During the holidays, the zoo lights up with hundreds of thousands of colorful bulbs for the annual Lights Before Christmas display.

The Zoo is located three miles from downtown Toledo on the Anthony Wayne Trail. It is open year round.

Parks & Natural Areas

◆ There are nine Metroparks in the Toledo area — nearly 7,000 acres of natural beauty, from unspoiled prairies to sand dunes, meadows and forests. The parks are open to the public year around, 7 a.m. to dark, free of charge. Oak Openings Preserve Metropark, west of Toledo, contains one of the best examples of oak savanna, a globally threatened habitat. Visitors may do a double take when they see the sand dunes in the woods, the remnants of a long-gone lake that preceded Lake Erie. Wildwood Preserve Metropark, on West Central Avenue in Toledo, is home to a 1938 Georgian Colonial mansion, the Manor House, which was built by R.A. Stranahan, an industrial pioneer and co-founder of Champion Spark Plug Co.

◆ Toledo Botanical Gardens, on Elmer Drive, is a city of Toledo park and a center for horticulture and the arts.

Metroparks of the Toledo Area

Ohio's only "living" sand dunes are located at Oak Openings Preserve Metropark, west of Toledo.

◆ Sprawling Ottawa Park, which stretches from Monroe Street near downtown to Bancroft Street near the University of Toledo, is the city's version of Central Park.

The Western Frontier

Fort Meigs, a log-and-earth fortification overlooking the Maumee River, became the focal point of the War of 1812 a year after it began. Here, the British suffered their first setback of the Northwest Campaign when a detachment of American troops stood up to combined forces of British and Canadian soldiers and Tecumseh's Indian warriors.

Located on State Route 65 in Perrysburg, Fort Meigs is the largest walled fortification in North America. General William Henry Harrison began building the fort in February, 1813, eight months after the United States declared war on Great Britain. Two months later, Shawnee Chief Tecumseh and his Indians surrounded the fort and on May 1, British troops from Fort Malden in Canada attacked. That siege lasted for a month, with the British retreating only after American reinforcements arrived from Kentucky.

Another siege in July lasted just a week before the British moved on to attack Fort Stephenson in nearby Fremont, another failure after which they returned to Canada.

Today, several blockhouses at the fort feature exhibits and dioramas on the War of 1812, the construction and reconstruction of the fort, and the lives of the soldiers who garrisoned Fort Meigs during the war. Visitors can view a six-pound cannon and the

Fort Meigs, built during the War of 1812, is the largest walled fortification in North America.

General Anthony Wayne and the Legion of the United States, pictured here in a reenactment, defeated a confederacy of natives at Fallen Timbers.

implements used to fire it, as well as the second-floor gun ports where soldiers took aim at the enemy.

On the Grand Battery, you can stand where General Harrison did when he watched as members of the Kentucky militia were trapped and taken prisoner on the opposite bank of the Maumee River. A stone shelter built by the Works Progress Administration in the 1930s serves as a visitor center and sales area. The park that surrounds the fort is open for picnics during daylight hours. The fort often hosts reenactments and encampments, as well as fife-and-drum concerts and demonstrations of cannon and musket firing.

Another history-making skirmish took place across the river 19 years earlier. On a hill overlooking the Maumee, several miles upriver, stands a landmark to the 1794 Battle of Fallen Timbers, a bloody confrontation between 900 US soldiers under the command of General "Mad" Anthony Wayne and 2,000 Indians backed by the British. The battle, which took place amid trees toppled by a tornado, ended the bloody Indian Wars. It has been called one of the three most significant battles in US history and is sometimes referred to as the last battle of the American Revolution. Fallen Timbers opened the entire region, including the Western Reserve, for settlement. Two years later, the city of Cleveland was plotted, and nine years later Ohio became a state.

The exact location of the Fallen Timbers Battlefield was not where the monument now stands, but across US 24. The battlefield was discovered in 1995 in a farm field surrounded by development and amazingly much of it was still intact. A consortium of agencies led by Metroparks of the Toledo Area has begun to acquire the property and will maintain it as an affiliate of the National Park Service. In time, Fallen Timbers could be recognized as Toledo's most significant historic site and is bound to become a national attraction.

The Miami & Erie Canal

An important piece of Ohio and Lake Erie history comes alive at Providence Metropark where The Volunteer, a mule-drawn replica of a late 1800s canal boat, operates on a reconstructed stretch of the original Miami and Erie Canal. Located across the Maumee River from the canal town of Grand Rapids, Ohio, west of Toledo on US Route 24, the boat passes through one of the original locks in the Cincinnati-to-Lake Erie water route. The boat crew is made up of historic interpreters in period clothing who stay in character for much of the 45-minute cruise. Park visitors can also tour the restored Isaac Ludwig Historic Mill and learn how waterpower is used to cut wood and grind flour. A general store

Metroparks of the Toledo Area

Visitors to Providence Metropark west of Toledo can step back in time to an era when travel was at the speed of plodding mules.

sells homespun crafts and souvenirs. Further upriver, at the western end of the park, is a roller dam that creates a slackwater pool and feeds water into the canal.

The Old West End

Listed in the National Register of Historic Places, the Old West End neighborhood represents the largest concentration of urban residential Victorian architecture in Ohio. Rosary Cathedral, in the heart of the neighborhood, is the primary church of the Roman Catholic Diocese of Toledo. The Cathedral of the Queen of the Most Holy Rosary is Spanish Plateresque in design, the only one of its kind in North America. Guided tours of the cathedral may be arranged through the Parish office on Collingwood Boulevard.

The Arts

◆ The century-old Toledo Museum of Art holds one of America's finest art collections, featuring works by the likes of El Greco, Rubens, Rembrandt, Van Gogh, Matisse and Picasso. Not surprisingly, the Glass City's museum also has one of the finest glass collections in the world. Other treasures in the collection are from ancient Egypt, Greece and Rome and there is a whole room from a French chateau. Paintings, glass sculpture, furniture, silver, tapestries and graphic arts are all represented in this expansive collection. The University of Toledo Center for the Visual Arts is located next door. Both are on Monroe Street. The Peristyle, part of the museum, is home to the Toledo Symphony Orchestra.

◆ The Valentine Theater is old and new. The 1890s theater on North Superior Street is a 900-seat performing arts venue which was renovated in the 1990s.

◆ The Ohio Theatre on Lagrange Street, built in 1921 for vaudeville shows, is now a non-profit performing arts center presenting family shows and educational programs.

◆ The Toledo Repertoire Theatre has brought community theater to Toledo since the 1930s. Productions are staged at its

The Valentine Theater, built in the 1890s, is a performing arts venue which was renovated in the 1990s.

quaint Tenth Street theater and at the Valentine, where "A Christmas Carol" is an annual tradition. The Rep hosts a Midwestern Playwrights Festival in April, which showcases a world premier by a regional playwright.

Sports

Toledo may not have the major league teams of its nearest big city neighbor, Detroit, but it has certainly made a name for itself in the minor leagues.

◆ The Mud Hens baseball team is a single-A farm club of the Detroit Tigers organization. It is easily the best known name in all of minor league sports. That reputation is partly thanks to the publicity the team received on the TV sit-com M*A*S*H, whose campy, cross-dressing Corporal Maxwell Klinger was played by Toledo native Jamie Farr. The Hens' season runs April through September. Home games are played at Ned Skeldon Stadium at the Lucas County Recreation Center in Maumee, but ground has been broken for a new "Hen House" in Toledo's downtown warehouse district, adjacent to the SeaGate Convention Center.

◆ The Toledo Storm hockey team is the East Coast Hockey League's affiliate to the National Hockey League's Detroit Red Wings. It is the latest in a long line of teams that have put Toledo on the map for the rough and tumble antics of minor league hockey. The season starts in October. Home games are played at the Toledo Sports Arena, on Main Street, on the east side of the river.

Art Weber Photo

The Toledo Mud Hens are possibly the most famous name in minor league sports.

◆ Top-notch private and public golf courses are located in Toledo, including city-owned Ottawa Park, rated by USA Today as one of the top 25 public courses in the nation. The private Inverness Club has hosted a PGA Tournament and Highland Meadows Golf Club is host of an annual Jamie Farr Ladies Professional Golf Association tournament. The Visitor and Convention Bureau has a guide to Toledo area courses.

◆ Toledo is also home to an annual, nationally televised Professional Bowling Association tournament.

◆ From a glass-enclosed grandstand, harness racing fans can enjoy the thrill of the hoofbeats year round at Raceway Park on Telegraph Road.

Other Attractions

◆ The green and blue building on the riverfront is the Center Of Science and Industry, or COSI, on Summit street. COSI features a variety of hands-on exhibits such as Mind Zone, which includes a distorted gravity room; Sports! where you can play a game of virtual volleyball, and Life Force, where visitors can explore the mysteries of their own bodies. Special exhibits change four times a year.

◆ Tony Packo's Cafe, home of the Hungarian hot dogs made famous by TV's Corporal Klinger, is the centerpiece of Toledo's Birmingham Ethnic Neighborhood.

The Center Of Science and Industry, COSI, features hands-on exhibits, including a distorted gravity room.

Shopping

◆ Toledo has four major shopping malls: Southwyck, on Reynolds Road at Glendale Avenue; Franklin Park, on Monroe Street; North Towne Square, on Alexis Road, and Woodville, on State Route 51 east of town. A new shopping center, the Mall at Fallen Timbers, is being planned off US 24 in Maumee, west of Toledo.

◆ Toledo Farmer's Market and the Erie Street Market are located in the Warehouse District at the corner of Market and Huron streets downtown. The Farmer's Market was recently renovated and the indoor Erie Street Market opened in 1997. It includes a new Libbey Glass factory outlet, specialty food stores, restaurants, and antiques.

Festivals

Besides the holiday festivals at Prominade Park, Toledo hosts a First Night celebration, an alcohol-free extravaganza with activities throughout downtown and fireworks at midnight to usher in the New Year. Ethnic festivals are a given in a town as diverse as Toledo. Hungarian, Greek, German and Polish festivals are held annually. The German-American Festival Society even maintains permanent festival grounds, Oak Shade Grove, in suburban Oregon. The annual Birmingham Ethnic Festival in August is a huge one-day celebration that combines several church festivals in the historic Birmingham Hungarian neighborhood centered around

Tony Packo's Café on the city's east side.

CIRCLE TOUR: The circle tour continues on I-75 north to Detroit, about an hour's drive away. The Monroe area is about halfway in between.

Southeast Michigan

"War" may not be the best description of the events of 1835. A shouting match would be more accurate. Militia from Ohio and Michigan faced off across the border prepared to do battle. It was the culmination of more than a decade of bickering about which state owned Toledo and the prosperity it promised as the northern terminus of the Miami and Erie Canal.

If the Toledo "War" had ended differently, the Glass City would be part of the Wolverine State today. As it turned out, Toledo remained in Ohio and the federal government gave Michigan the Upper Peninsula as part of the deal. Not a single shot was fired and the only casualties were a few bruised egos — not all that different from the annual Ohio State-Michigan football game today.

Crossing the border from Ohio to Michigan on I-75 is a lot less eventful these days. A quick exit at Luna Pier, Michigan, is the first stop to see Lake Erie from the Michigan shore. The small community has a long, crescent-shaped pier that's worth a walk. A small park is an inviting place for a picnic, and benches along the pier offer spots to sit and watch fishermen in spring, or duck hunters just off shore in the fall. A Michigan Welcome Center greets northbound travelers between Luna Pier and Monroe.

Historic Monroe

History is everywhere in Monroe, the largest Michigan city near the Ohio border and one of the oldest communities in the state. Monroe is the adoptive hometown of General George Custer

The pier at Lune Pier is a pleasant place to rest or stretch along the Michigan shore of Lake Erie.

and the site of one of the bloodiest battles of the War of 1812. The small town offers big shopping options nearby, including a factory outlet mall and a new Cabela's outdoor outfitter store said to be the largest of its kind in the world.

The area may be best known, however, for its innovations in manufacturing products that have made our lives more comfortable. Monroe County, located along the I-75 auto-manufacturing corridor, is home to Monroe Auto Equipment, maker of the Monroe brand shock absorber, an auto part that was invented here and has been smoothing out the bumps in the road ever since. The most famous product to come out of Monroe, though, is the beloved reclining chair, the invention that is the nucleus of the La-Z-Boy Chair Co. The Fortune 500 furniture maker still maintains its corporate headquarters here.

Two icons of western Lake Erie can be seen on the horizon near Monroe. Detroit Edison's 1,139-megawatt Fermi 2 plant is one of three nuclear power plants on Lake Erie. Fermi's twin, hourglass-shaped cooling towers are easily seen from the beach at Maumee Bay State Park on the Ohio shore and from miles out on the lake. The smokestacks of the company's nearby Monroe Power Plant have been fixtures of western Lake Erie for decades. The enormous coal-fired electric generating plant is one of the largest fossil fuel plants in the U.S., generating 3,000 megawatts of power.

Cabela's

Cabela's, "The World's Foremost Outfitter," opened its newest and largest retail outlet in 2000 in the small town of Dundee, west of Monroe. The 225,000-square-foot store, which resembles a huge hunting lodge and has a 20-foot sculpture of wrestling grizzly bears out front, contains nearly every item found in the company's internationally known catalog of outdoor gear.

Situated halfway between Toledo and Detroit in a state known for its outdoor recreation, the outdoor super-store is expected to attract up to six million visitors a year, which would make it the single largest tourist attraction in the state. Cabela's is located at the intersection of US 23 and M50, about 30 miles from either Toledo or Detroit.

The Monroe area was already a shopping destination before Cabela's came to the region. The Horizon Outlet Center is a major attraction, with more than 40 outlets stores, some selling national brand name clothing and housewares. The mall is located just off I-75 at LaPlaisance Road, and is the center of a growing commercial strip that includes restaurants, hotels and a campground.

Cabela's opened its newest and largest retail outlet in the small town of Dundee, west of Monroe.

The Raisin River Battlefield Visitors Center holds special events throughout the year to commemorate the battle that took place there during the War of 1812.

"Remember the Raisin"

The War of 1812 capped 60 years of conflict that began with the French and Indian War in the 1750s, through the Revolution and another 30 years of skirmishes with the Indians. In 1812, the war hawks in Congress became angry that the British had seized American cargo ships overseas during the Napoleonic War there. The affront to American commerce coupled with an alliance between the British and Indians on the American border in Upper Canada (Ontario) fostered an atmosphere of paranoia. America was at war again.

The War of 1812 was unpopular from the start. Several New England states even refused to participate. Militia members — practically every able-bodied man — were less than enthusiastic about leaving their crops in the fields to fight a battle with Canadians, many of whom were Americans gone north for new opportunities. Then there were the early defeats. Almost a month after Congress declared war, British and Indian troops surrounded Fort Mackinaw in Michigan and captured it without a single shot being fired. The British had the major advantage of knowing there was a war going on, since word had not yet reached the ill-fated soldiers at Fort Mackinaw. A month later, General William Hull marched his Ohio Militia troops up from Dayton with the intention of taking Fort Malden near Windsor. Not only did he fail to gain ground, but lost Detroit in the process.

That brings us to Frenchtown, now known as Monroe, and the River Raisin Battlefield Visitor Center on Elm Ave. The center uses exhibits, an audio-visual presentation, and living history to tell the story of one of the bloodiest battles ever staged on American soil.

Frenchtown was located along the River Raisin, or Riviere aux Raisins, named for the white grapes that once covered the trees and bushes along the banks. During the war the Raisin was considered by British-Canadians as the international boundary, which would keep almost all of the Great Lakes in the northern territory.

British troops and Indians lead by the powerful Shawnee chief Tecumseh massacred settlers and Kentucky militiamen at Frenchtown in a battle that began in the early morning hours of January 22, 1813. It was a vicious attack; only 33 of the 934 Americans escaped being captured or killed. Some lay wounded from the battle when the Indians returned the next day and burnt the town to the ground. It was early in the Northwest campaign and the bitter defeat would linger in the memories of the Americans for the remainder of the war. "Remember the Raisin" was the battle cry later that year when the Americans met Tecumseh and his warriors again near the Thames River in Ontario, a battle that would be Tecumseh's last.

By some accounts, the War of 1812 was a draw. In the end, the international boundaries even went back to the way they were. But the war did seal Canada's independence from the United States, the US's sovereignty from Europe was once and for all established, and neither was challenged again.

The Raisin River Battlefield Visitors Center holds special events throughout the year to commemorate the battle and the war.

Historic reenactors paddle to shore during Old Frenchtown Days in Monroe, Michigan.

The annual Old French Town Days in late August in Monroe is a major historical festival with reenactments, canoe races, tomahawk throws, music and crafts.

Other Historic Sites

◆ A monument called "Sighting the Enemy," depicting George Armstrong Custer astride his beloved horse, Dandy, stands at Monroe Street and Elm Avenue. The young cavalry leader and Gettysburg veteran, who was born in Ohio and grew up in Monroe, was a controversial figure who is most famous for his death at age 37 in the 1876 Battle of Little Big Horn. The general's widow, Elizabeth, was present, along with President William Taft, when the statue was unveiled in 1910.

◆ Monroe also has two war memorials. The Korean War Memorial, on North Custer Road west of Telegraph Road, is situated along the River Raisin. A Vietnam Veterans Memorial at Heck Park on N. Dixie Highway, south of I-75, incorporates Huey and Cobra helicopters, a Walk of Freedom and a memorial etched with the names of local men killed in the war, reminiscent of the national monument in Washington D.C.

◆ Navarre Anderson Trading Complex, North Custer Road in Raisinville Township, focuses primarily on the War of 1812. The complex includes a building that is the oldest surviving wooden structure in Michigan and considered one of the best examples of "piece-sur-piece" construction in the Old Northwest. The building has been restored to its 1797 appearance, when it was home to

The Vietnam Veterans Memorial in Monroe is reminiscent of the larger memorial in Washington, DC.

Peter Navarre, the son of one of the area's first settlers, who became a famous woodsman and scout during the War of 1812.

♦ The Monroe County Historical Museum, 126 South Monroe Street, has collections focusing on early Monroe, General Custer, Indian lore and life in the 1800s.

Sterling State Park

From the marsh trail at Sterling State Park you can hear the cries of gulls above the distant rumble of traffic on I-75, the hum of high-tension electric wires overhead and the distant whistle of a factory sounding shift change. The park, which is scheduled for a major overhaul, has a nature museum, 192 campsites, a boat launch, picnic areas and a fishing access. It is Michigan's only state park on Lake Erie and a pleasant retreat just off the interstate. Sterling is located at the mouth of the Raisin River on Dixie Highway (I-75 Exit 15). Michigan charges admission to its state parks.

CIRCLE TOUR: The Circle Tour leaves I-75 to follow M-85 north through Detroit's "Downriver" suburbs before returning to I-75 at the Detroit City limits.

The Detroit River

Lake Erie is connected to the upper Great Lakes by a straight pipe that bulges in the center. Water from Lake Huron flows down the St. Clair River to Lake St. Clair, then funnels into the Detroit River for the final 32-mile stretch to Lake Erie. Every boat traveling between the upper and lower Great Lakes, including freighters from 100 world ports, passes through the d'etroit, or "the straight," as French explorers called it.

The river is also the conduit for up to half the hawks in North America, which follow the stream south during fall migration. For that reason, Lake Erie Metropark is a good place to stand waiting on a crisp autumn day with binoculars pressed to your face. The

A merlin is a small hawk, sometimes called a pigeon hawk, that is an occasional visitor to Lake Erie during spring and fall migrations.

park at the mouth of the Detroit River, near Rockwood north of Monroe, is one of the best places on the continent to view migrating hawks such as turkey vultures, sharp-shinned hawks, red-tailed hawks, American kestrels and northern harriers. It's possible to see all 16 species that frequent the river corridor in a single autumn afternoon when the big birds pass through, riding columns of air heated by the sun. Mostly, though, you will see broad-winged hawks.

In 1999 — September 18 to be exact — birders assembled for an annual Hawk Watch Festival at the park saw more broad-winged hawks than they could accurately count, but 500,000 was the conservative estimate. Not all of the hawks that spend the summer in Canadian breeding grounds funnel down the river; some follow the Atlantic coast south. But in 1999, with Hurricane Floyd parked off the eastern seaboard, more birds than usual were forced to follow the Detroit River route. The half-million "broadwings" seen that day was a North American record that boosted the area's reputation as a hot spot for hawks.

An organization called Southeastern Michigan Raptor Research, which sponsors the Hawk Watch Festival and conducts the annual count, monitors the Metropark and neighboring Pointe Mouilee State Game Area to learn more about the raptor migration. Daily-updated counts are posted at the Mashlands Museum and Nature Center, located in the park.

Lake Erie Metropark, part of the Huron-Clinton Metropark system, which surrounds Detroit, has a marina and boat launch, a wave action swimming pool, an 18-hole golf course, a large

A great egret stalks the waters at Pointe Mouilee.

playground and picnic areas, some overlooking the river. The park is located on West Jefferson Road. (I-75 Exit 29A). There is an admission fee.

The Pointe Mouilee state game area at the end of Campau Road, next to the Lake Erie Metropark golf course, is an active place, especially in the evening when fishermen mingle with birders and boaters at this incomparable access to the Detroit River mouth. Late Woodland Indians settled here because they were attracted by the abundant wildlife. The French fur traders who came later looking for beaver pelts gave the area its very accurate name, which means "wet point." In 1875, wealthy sportsmen organized the Big Eight Shooting Club on the site, which the Michigan Department of Conservation acquired in 1945. In the 1980s, dredge material from the Detroit River was used to restore the Pointe.

Trenton and Grosse Ile

About 20 miles upriver, on M-85, Elizabeth Park in the city of Trenton offers sweeping views of the Detroit River, as well as access to the shore for fishing, picnicking, or just lazing by the bank. The historic park — the oldest in Wayne County, which includes all of Detroit — has a transient marina, handicap fishing access, old buildings where pigeons perch in the rafters, food concessions and even pony rides for the kids.

Arched bridges are a distinctive feature of Elizabeth Park in Trenton, Michigan.

Near the entrance to the park is a swing bridge leading to Grosse Ile (pronounced "ill" or "eel"), the largest of a group of islands in the Detroit River occupied by about 10,000 residents. La grosse Ile, "the large island," as early French explorers called it, is actually two islands divided by a canal. There are more than a dozen islands, some of which are inhabited by people, others only by birds and other wildlife. Two bridges connect the main island with the mainland. One is free to cross, while the other, privately owned span, charges a small toll.

Grosse Ile has been inhabited since Detroit businessmen purchased it from the Potawatomi Indians in 1876. Several of Detroit's automotive pioneers had summer homes here, including R.E. Olds (Oldsmobile), Charles and William Fisher (Fisher Body), and General William S. Knudsen (General Motors). Henry Ford and his wife owned a large piece of property. The Fords never built a home of their own there, but sold land to several Ford Motor Co. executives who did. The island was a navy seaplane base in the 1920s and American and British pilots trained here during World War II.

The Grosse Ile Lighthouse, built in 1894 and rebuilt in 1906, guided ships on the river for the first half of the century. It has not operated since 1940. A handful of homes built in the 1840s to 1860s make up a National Historic District on East River at Parkway. An 1867 Episcopal church is also listed on the National Register of Historic places, while a dozen 1920s era homes are listed on Michigan's historic register. A railroad depot that now serves as a historical museum may seem out of place on the island. The railroad bridges that once crossed the river connecting the U.S. and Canada are long gone.

On to Detroit

I-75 leaves suburbia and plunges into a sea of industry that seems to stretch forever on either side of the Interstate. It is a mass of pipes, towers and tanks that lights up at night like a large city seen from an airplane. A little farther, the first glimpse of downtown comes into view — distant skyscrapers amid a tangle of busy highways befitting a place known as the Motor City.

Prominent on the skyline, before downtown, are the familiar towers of the Ambassador Bridge, which reaches 9,600 feet across the Detroit River and the international border where this journey began. Even with the end of the Circle Tour in sight, the largest city on Lake Erie is still ahead.

More Information

Cabela's-Dundee
110 Cabela Blvd. East
Dundee, MI 48131
734-529-4700
www.cabelas.com

Greater Toledo Convention & Visitors Bureau
401 Jefferson Avenue
Toledo, OH 43604-1067
1-800-243-4667
www.toledocvb.com

Monroe County Convention & Tourism Bureau
106 W. Front Street, Suite C
Monroe, MI 48161
1-800-252-3011
www.monroeinfo.com

Toledo Metroparks
5100 W. Central Ave.
Toledo, OH 43615
419-535-3050
www.metroparkstoledo.com

Toledo Zoo
PO Box 4010, 2700 Broadway
Toledo, OH 43609
419-385-5721
www.toledozoo.org

**Statues in the outfield of Detroit's new
Comerica Park pay tribute to Tiger legends.**

CIRCLE TOUR: *The Circle Tour continues north through the
Detroit suburbs of Wyandotte and Lincoln Park. At the Detroit city
limits, the tour rejoins I-75 north to the Ambassador Bridge exit,
and continues on to Windsor. To get to downtown Detroit, stay on
I-75 north and exit at the John C. Lodge Freeway.*

Chapter 11

Detroit

A n afternoon Tigers game is just breaking up and throngs of people are fanning out in all directions from Comerica Park. Many are headed to Greek Town or across Woodward Avenue to the Hockeytown Café, where they mingle with the crowd waiting for the first show to begin at the Second City Comedy Club or a concert at The Fox Theatre next door.

Police officers direct traffic at intersections as motorists find their way through the maze of streets to the jumble of highways, where most head north to the suburbs. But even as baseball fans funnel out of downtown, gamblers stream into the city's new gaming palaces where the night is just beginning.

The scene belies Detroit's reputation as a place where nobody wants to go. Newspaper and television stories only a few years ago depicted the Motor City as a crime-ridden, Rust Belt town — a scary place best to avoid. Detroit, they said, wasn't what she used to be. But headlines today tell a different story of a 300-year-old city with new ideas about its future.

Billions of dollars are being invested in Detroit's downtown in an unprecedented period of revitalization. Next door to Comerica

***The Renaissance Center, or RenCen,
towers over the Detroit skyline.***

Park, Ford Field, the new domed den for the Lions, was still under construction as the city made a successful bid to host the Super Bowl there in 2006. Three opulent casinos were open in converted old buildings awaiting construction to begin on their permanent homes on the riverfront, where a major transformation is already under way.

Presiding over all this is the Renaissance Center, a 73-story fortress of glass and steel surrounded by six smaller towers. The building, built in 1977, dominates the skyline and anchors the new riverfront development spearheaded by its new owner, General Motors. GM purchased the "RenCen" in 1996 and began to sink $500 million into the building and its surroundings. Plans call for a five-story glass-enclosed public area called the Winter Garden overlooking Detroit's historic river and ground-level retail stores to create an inviting marketplace. Work has already begun on a state-funded riverfront promenade, a landscape-lined granite walkway from the RenCen to Joe Louis Arena, where the Red Wings play. GM also plans to extend the promenade east of the RenCen and convert parking lots into retail and office space.

Eventually, the new casinos will line up on the riverfront alongside a new Tricentennial State Park, creating a chain of new development and greenways stretching from the Belle Isle Bridge to the Ambassador Bridge.

That is only a sample of what is happening in Motown these days. People and money are pouring into downtown. No, Detroit isn't what she used to be.

From a Cadillac to a Ford

Detroit is the grand old lady of the Great Lakes — one of the largest and oldest cities in the Midwest. Its metropolitan area of nearly 5 million people is among the ten largest in the U.S.

Explorer Antoine de la Mothe Cadillac and his party of about 100 landed on a narrow spot on the Detroit River in 1701 where they established a strategic outpost that would allow the French to control all water-borne commerce between the upper and lower Great Lakes. Sixty years later, the British captured the town during the French and Indian War and used it as a fort during the Revolution. It became part of the United States in the treaty that followed Anthony Wayne's victory at the Battle of Fallen Timbers near Toledo. The town burned to the ground in the early 1800s and was captured by the British for a while in the War of 1812. Three years later it became a city; 22 years later Michigan became a state.

Fast forward to 1896, less than 100 years after Cadillac's landing, when Henry Ford rolled his first automobile out of a tool shed in Detroit. Within seven years the Ford Motor Company was born and Detroit — indeed, the world — would become a different place.

Ford didn't invent the automobile, but he might as well have. His company's Model T, which debuted in 1908, was dubbed the "universal car" and became the first low-cost, reliable mode of transportation for a country on the move. The company sold 10,660 of the "Lizzies," as fans called them, in the first year of production, beginning a new era of mobility.

Ten years after Ford and 11 associates started their car company in a converted wagon shop with 10 employees and $28,000, Ford was producing half the automobiles in the United Sates. To keep up with the demand, Ford initiated mass production in his factory, with each worker remaining in one assigned place with one task to do as the automobile moved from station to station. By the time the assembly line was perfected, Model T's rolled out of the factory at the rate of one every 10 seconds.

Ford's other major innovation came in 1914 when he announced that Ford Motor Company's minimum wage would increase to $5 a day—more than double the existing minimum rate. His theory was simple: If he paid his workers well, they could afford to buy the cars they made. In 19 years, more than 15 million Fords were cruising new roads all across the country.

Today, as the company approaches its centennial, the Ford family of companies and affiliated automakers produce 70 different models of cars and trucks under the names Ford, Lincoln, Mercury, Volvo, Mazda, Jaguar, Aston Martin and Land Rover. Henry Ford, Fortune Magazine's "Businessman of the Century," may not have invented the automobile, but as the company history says, "his Model T started a rural revolution, his $5 a day pay scale started a social revolution and his moving assembly line started an industrial revolution." In the process, he put Detroit on the map as carmaker to the world. Today, the Motor City is home not only to Ford, but the headquarters of General Motor Corporation, DaimlerChrysler and Volkswagen of America.

Buoyed by the infusion of auto money, The Roaring Twenties was Detroit's heyday. In that era the city's impressive skyline took shape — the General Motors Building, the Fisher Building, the Detroit Public Library, Henry Ford Museum and Greenfield Village, and the Ambassador Bridge. Now, a new heyday looms for Detroit, where the names of the carmakers are still associated with progress. Ford Field, the football stadium, will play a key role in downtown's rebirth and lure the Lions back home from the suburbs. New auto museums funded by Ford and Chrysler are attracting tourists. And of course there is the renovation of the Renaissance Center, where General Motors, maker of the Cadillac, runs its worldwide operations just a few hundred yards from the very spot where Cadillac the explorer first came ashore.

Progress," Henry Ford said in 1923, "consists in a number of related things changing together for the better." He could have been talking about Detroit today. Ford also said: "The unhappiest man on earth is the one who has nothing to do." If that is the case, there should be no unhappy people in Motown these days.

Three of a Kind

Spelled out in red lights, the words WINDSOR CASINO beckon Americans to come across the border and bring their cash. Separated only by the river, Windsor is not so much like another country as an extension of Detroit, just over the bridge. When the casino opened, Detroit enjoyed some of the success the giant tourist magnet was pulling in, but the real money was just out of reach. That is until 1999 when Detroit stepped up to the gambling table. In the battle for bettors, the bigger city wasn't about to fold, and Motown beat Windsor's ace with three of a kind.

Detroit's first casino, MGM Grand, celebrated its first anniversary in 2000 with booming business and revenue second only to MGM's Las Vegas casino. The MotorCity Casino opened next and also performed beyond expectations. The new casinos stripped Casino Windsor of some of its business, but the Canadian casino has continued to lead the pack in revenue partly because of an exchange rate that favors the American dollar. Detroit's third casino opened in the fall of 2000 in the famous Greektown district.

The three casinos on the Detroit side of the river all operate out of temporary quarters until a new strip complete with a large entertainment venue is built along the riverfront. (The most recent target opening date is 2004.) These temporary casinos, though, are far from second rate. Each of them has row after row of slot machines and up to 200 game tables, plus restaurants, lounges and valet parking. Each is open around the clock.

The MGM Grand was the first of three casinos in downtown Detroit.

Metropolitan Detroit Convention & Visitors Bureau

The MGM Grand, which (ironically) occupies a former Internal Revenue Service office building, features a classic Hollywood theme with a red and gold exterior and has three upscale restaurants. MotorCity, located in an abandoned Wonder Bread factory, has an urban, art deco interior and nightclub atmosphere. Greektown, the most lavish of the three, has a Mediterranean theme meant to blend with the surrounding entertainment district.

With four casinos, the Detroit-Windsor area has quickly become the gambling Mecca of the Midwest — the major casino center between Las Vegas and Atlantic City. And it's only beginning. The permanent casinos on the Detroit side, which will come with about 2,600 new hotel rooms, are expected to attract 5 million to 7 million new visitors a year.

Henry Ford Museum & Greenfield Village

In 1912, Henry Ford began buying agricultural equipment, power machinery and early "horseless carriages," keenly (perhaps uniquely) aware of their historic significance. Today Ford's collection is one of Michigan's largest tourist attractions, the Henry Ford Museum and Greenfield Village in suburban Dearborn. With holdings of more than one million objects and 26 million documents, prints and photographs, it is the largest indoor/outdoor historical complex in the world.

Ford and Edward Cutler, a Ford Motor Company engineer, spent two decades restoring the pieces and building the "antique village." In 1929, with President Herbert Hoover and many of the most respected scientists, industrialists and celebrities of the day on hand, Henry Ford dedicated the Edison Institute Museum & Greenfield Village to his long-time friend Thomas Edison. The museum was renamed for Ford in 1953, after his death.

Everything from toasters to tractors is on display at the museum. The exhibit "100 Years of the Automobile in American Life" takes visitors on a journey through the evolution of the motorcar. The exhibit includes more than 100 cars and thousands of other artifacts, from a 1940s roadside diner to a 1960s Holiday Inn room. The eclectic collection also includes everything from the chair Abraham Lincoln was sitting in when he was assassinated to

The Automobile in American Life Exhibit is one of the most memorable displays at the Henry Ford Museum & Greenfield Village.

Metropolitan Detroit Convention & Visitors Bureau

Edgar Allan Poe's writing desk. Vehicles in the museum range from President Kennedy's limousine to newsman Charles Kuralt's "On the Road" tour van to the Oscar Mayer "Wienermobile."

Greenfield Village is a full-scale museum of American life. Among the collection of buildings are the home Henry Ford was born in, an 1850s stagecoach stop, Edison's Menlo Park Laboratory and the Logan County Courthouse where Lincoln argued cases as a traveling "circuit" rider in Postville, Illinois. The house where Noah Webster finished the first American Dictionary, and the Wright Brothers' Cycle Shop are also part of this fantasy, historical neighborhood.

Homage to the Automobile

Car nuts must be crazy about Detroit. Besides the Henry Ford Museum, numerous other museums pay tribute to the region's automaking tradition and the lives of the auto barons. And each winter, the world's auto industry focuses on Cobo Hall, home of an international auto show.

◆ The Automotive Hall of Fame, recently relocated to the Henry Ford Museum campus in Dearborn, uses interactive exhibits and a large-screen theater to tell the story of the automobile and challenge visitors' creativity. At one exhibit, you can even identify your own character traits and match them with people in the museum. Who knows, you may discover you have a lot in common with Dr. Ferdinand Porsche or Soichiro Honda.

◆ The Walter P. Chrysler Museum near DaimlerChryslers' North American headquarters in Auburn Hills (an hour north of Detroit) has about 75 vehicles on display from vintage cars to concept vehicles.

◆ GM World is a display of new and historic automobiles in a museum-like setting located in the company's world headquarters at the Renaissance Center downtown.

◆ Another auto-related attraction on Ford's growing Dearborn campus is the Sprit of Ford, a high-tech interactive exhibit that gives a behind-the-scenes look at how Ford vehicles are designed and built. From a design studio to a wind tunnel to a race track, theme park-like exhibits take visitors through the process of building a car from concept to completion. Guests also perform pit stop maintenance on a racecar, watch a crash test, and learn about the high-tech aspects of today's automobiles such as aerodynamics and fuel efficiency.

◆ Edsel & Eleanor Ford House, located on 87 acres along Lake St. Clair (north of Detroit in Grosse Pointe Shores) is the mansion where Ford's son and his wife raised their four children. It is open for public tours.

◆ The Fisher Mansion, home of Lawrence Fisher, founder of the Fisher Body Company and Cadillac Motors, is located on Lenox Drive on the riverfront in Detroit. Alfred Brush Ford, great-grandson of Henry Ford, bought the home in 1975 and turned it

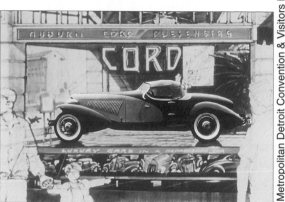

A showroom from the 1930s is among the exhibits at the Auto Hall of Fame in Dearborn.

Metropolitan Detroit Convention & Visitors Bureau

into the Bhaktivedanta Cultural Center devoted to India's heritage and philosophy. It is open May through September.

◆ Henry Ford Estate-Fair Lane, the 56-room Scottish Baronial home Henry Ford built in 1914 along the Rouge River in Dearborn, is a self-sufficient estate with its own powerplant. The house, a National Historic Landmark, is located on the campus that includes the Henry Ford Museum and Automotive Hall of Fame. A self-guided walking tour takes in a tree house, boathouse, gardens, and scenic vistas.

◆ Meadow Brook Hall is a 100-room mansion built by John Dodge's widow, Matilda Dodge Wilson, and her second husband, Alfred Wilson. The 1929 mansion is considered one of the finest examples of residential architecture. The Wilsons founded Oakland University, which now occupies the 1,400-acre estate grounds. Public tours of the mansion include a 2/3-scale playhouse built for 12-year-old Frances Dodge. A classic car show is held here each August and the house is decorated during the holidays.

◆ For more than 80 years, automakers from around the world have been coming to Detroit's Cobo Hall in January to display their wares. The North American International Auto Show, sponsored by the Detroit Auto Dealers' Association, attracts more than 700,000 people and 5,000 media from around the world to see all the new models under one roof. Concept cars give a glimpse of what the cars of the future will look like. Over the years, the

Fair Lane is a 56-room Scottish Baronial home Henry Ford built in 1914 along the Rouge River in Dearborn.

Mark Arpin Photo, MDCVB

compact car, the sport utility vehicle and, more recently, alternative fuel cars have debuted at the show.

Hitsville USA

If Cleveland rocks, Detroit rolls. The city that gave us mass-produced cars also mass-produced the music that emanated from their dashboards in the 1960s. Credit Detroit for the simple pleasure of cruising to a catchy tune on a Saturday night.

In the late 1950s, when Detroit was building its system of modern highways, record producer Barry Gordy was building a new sound that would launch the careers of such enduring artists as Stevie Wonder and Marvin Gaye. Gordy bought a house at 2648 West Grand Boulevard, named it Hitsville USA, and built an empire with his skills as a songwriter and manager with the performing talents the likes of Diana Ross and the Supremes, the Jackson Five, Martha and the Vandellas, The Temptations and the Four Tops. As the business grew, Gordy bought more houses, eventually owning seven in the neighborhood at one time.

Today, two of those houses, including Hitsville USA, make up the Motown Historical Museum. Exhibits feature rare photos, gold records, artists' costumes and other memorabilia of the Motown era. The most popular exhibit is the studio where scores of hit records, from "Stop in the Name of Love" to "Dancin' in the Streets" to "My Girl," were recorded. Upstairs is Gordy's apartment, where he and his staff would spend long nights packing records for shipping.

Hitsville USA, the Motown Museum, preserves the humble recording studio where Barry Gordy made hits and stars.

More Music

The home of Motown is also the hometown of pop music icons from Bob Seger to Ted Nugent to rappers Kidd Rock and Eminem. Two of the city's largest annual events, however, center around two other musical genres:

◆ The Montreux Detroit Jazz Festival, the largest free jazz festival in North America, is held each Labor Day weekend and attracts more than 750,000 music fans to the Music Hall Center for the Performing Arts on Madison Avenue. The festival is broadcast across the country on National Public Radio.

◆ More than 800,000 country music fans turn out each May for the world's largest country music festival, the Downtown Hoedown, at Hart Plaza. In the past, the festival has featured such nationally known performers as Reba McIntyre and Garth Brooks.

Sports City

Detroit was named The Sporting News' "Best Sports City" in 1998, the year the Red Wings won the National Hockey League's Stanley Cup Championship for the second straight year. Eight years earlier, the Pistons were in the limelight after capturing the basketball equivalent of the feat, back-to-back National Basketball Association World Championships. Today, it's the Tigers and the Lions that have sports fans pumped, although the excitement has more to do with the teams' side-by-side stadiums downtown than their prowess on the playing field.

◆ Comerica Park opened for the 2000 baseball season. It was a bittersweet moment in sports because the home opener at Comerica marked the end of venerable Tiger Stadium at the corner of Michigan and Trumbull Avenues, the oldest baseball stadium still in use at the time. The new $240 million stadium is state-of-the-art, but it includes a few nods to tradition, including statues of Tigers greats along the outfield wall.

◆ Ford Field was still under construction as the Tigers finished their first season at Comerica next door. The $225 million domed stadium will lure the football team back to the city from the

*Comerica Park
in downtown
Detroit.*

Silverdome in Pontiac. It will also bring the Super Bowl to Detroit in 2006 and is large enough to host the Final Four or a national political convention.

◆ The Red Wings routinely pack the house at Joe Louis Arena near the riverfront. When tickets to the sold-out arena are hard to come by, the next best thing is a seat at the Hockeytown Café, a sports bar owned by Red Wings owner Olympia Entertainment. Hockeytown, where a sheet of ice lines the bar to keep your beer cold, is located in an entertainment complex next to the Fox Theatre and across the street from Comerica Park and Ford Field.

◆ The Pistons and the Detroit Shock of the Women's National Basketball Association both play at The Palace of Auburn Hills, an hour north of the city on I-75. The Palace is also home to the Vipers of the International Hockey League and the Fury of the Arena Football League.

◆ The Detroit Rockers professional indoor soccer team plays most of its home games at the Compuware Sports Arena in Plymouth, which is also home to the Plymouth Whalers minor league hockey team.

◆ The American Power Boat Association's Gold Cup hydroplane race attracts the largest single-day crowd for a sporting event in the United States. Up to 500,000 people line the banks of the Detroit River to see the racing boats reach speeds of up to 225 mph. The APBA Gold Cup has been called the Indy 500 of boat racing.

The Red Wings always sell out Cobo Hall in "Hockeytown."

Mark Hicks Photo, MDCVB

◆ The Detroit Grand Prix is a three-day, world-class auto race at Belle Isle Park. The 2.36-mile street course with 14 turns is considered one of the most challenging in the world.

Downtown Motown

Getting around the city center is as simple as hopping aboard the People Mover at any of its 13 stations. The elevated computerized rail transit system makes a 2.9 mile circuit in 15 minutes, linking the city's major office buildings and attractions, from Cobo Center to the Renaissance Center to Greektown.

◆ One of the focal points of downtown is Hart Plaza, a riverfront park made up of sculptures and fountains where you can rest and watch the people and the riverboats go by. The plaza is the site of many of the city's major festivals, including an Ethnic Festival Series.

◆ Another important feature of downtown is Rivertown, a historic warehouse district stretching from the RenCen to the Belle Isle Bridge that has been renovated as a strip of restaurants and nightclubs with an outdoor amphitheater.

◆ The Eastern Market, on Gratiot Avenue at Russell Street, is the largest flower-bedding market in the world. For more than 110 years it has been the center of trade for farmers from Michigan, Ohio and Canada and handles goods from as far away as Europe, the Middle East, Asia and South America.

◆ Detroit's theaters are not only the venues for national touring acts, but architectural gems as well. Three were built in 1928: The Fisher Theatre in the Fisher Building on Grand Boulevard is a movie house designed to resemble a Mayan Temple. The lavish Fox Theatre on Woodward Avenue is an example of exotic Siamese Byzantine architecture and was modeled after an Arabian tent. The Music Hall Center for the Performing Arts on Madison Avenue was built by Matilda Dodge Wilson, widow of auto baron John F. Dodge, and has an art deco exterior and a Spanish Renaissance interior.

◆ The 1919 Orchestra Hall on Woodward, a National Historic Landmark, is home to the Detroit Symphony Orchestra and is nationally known for its acoustic qualities. The turn-of-the-century Gem Theatre has been undergoing a major restoration to restore its original Spanish revival grandeur.

Belle Isle

A family could take a min-vacation on Belle Isle, home to a zoo, an aquarium, a conservatory and a maritime museum. The 1,000-acre island in the Detroit River three miles from downtown is an urban oasis of memorials, fountains, athletic fields and manmade lagoons. It is a popular place for picnicking, fishing and jogging.

Known as *Wah-na-be-zee* (Swan Island) to the Chippewa and Ottawa tribes, the city bought the island in 1879. It was designed as a park in 1883 by famed landscape architect Frederick Law Olmstead, designer of New York's Central Park and Buffalo's chain of urban greenspaces. One of the shelters on the island is what remains of the Belle Isle Casino, once considered the finest casino in the United States. The island is reached by the MacArthur Bridge, which connects Belle Isle to East Grand Boulevard.

At the Belle Isle Zoo, owned by the Detroit Zoological Institute, visitors can view 47 species of animals from a 3/4-mile long elevated boardwalk overlooking the exhibits. An African lions exhibit and the World of Spiders are two of the most popular features. The zoo is open May through October.

The Dossin Great Lakes Museum on Belle Isle has the anchor of the S.S. Edmund Fitzgerald, the pilothouse from the freighter S.S. William Clay Ford and an extensive collection of model ships.

Metropolitan Detroit Convention & Visitors Bureau

The Belle Isle Aquarium, also operated by the Zoological Institute, is North America's oldest, continuously operating public aquarium, dating to 1904. Sixty exhibits with a total capacity of 32,000 gallons of water contain 1,500 individual animals of 146 species. Among them are native Detroit River species such as trout, bass, pike, perch and walleye. The aquarium is best known for successfully breeding and rearing freshwater stingrays. It is open year round.

The Whitcomb Conservatory, also built in 1904, houses the Palm House filled with tropical plants up to 85 feet tall. Orchids, southwest-American plants and ferns are part of the permanent collection, while six major flower displays are staged annually in the Show House. Formal gardens surround the Conservatory. It is open year round. Admission is free.

The Dossin Great Lakes Museum has the anchor of the S.S. Edmund Fitzgerald, the pilothouse from the freighter S.S. William Clay Ford and an extensive collection of model ships. The Gothic Room, full of carved oak, brass and stained glass, captures the heyday at the turn of the century passenger vessels, while another exhibit looks at the yachts owned by the auto barons of the 1920s and the 1930s.

Ethnic Heritage

African-Americans have a long and rich history in Detroit. Detroit was known as the North Star to fleeing slaves headed for the Canadian border before abolition and is the adoptive hometown of Rosa Parks, the embodiment of the civil rights movement in the south. It is also home to the largest museum devoted to African-American culture and history. The Charles H. Wright Museum of African-American History was built in 1997 at the Detroit Cultural Center on East Warren Street. The museum has more than 20,000 artifacts and archival materials.

Detroit is known for its diversity and has several major ethnic neighborhoods that are tourist destinations in their own right.

◆ Greektown is Detroit's most famous ethnic neighborhood. The two-block area on Monroe Street between Brush and the Chrysler Freeway service drive is an entertainment district with a wide variety of restaurants, nightclubs, bakeries, markets, shops and three historic churches. It is also home to one of the city's three new casinos. The Alley, a four-level festival marketplace located in a building that was a tannery in the late 19th century, features shops, restaurants and entertainment. An art festival is held here in May.

◆ The International Center Building, located in Greektown, is a renovated seed factory that now houses offices. An atrium in the building features the largest indoor waterfall in the world, tumbling 103 feet. The center is home to a Cajun-Creole restaurant called Fishbones Rhythm Kitchen and a 175-suite Anthem Suite Hotel and Conference center known for its eight-story mural depicting Greek gods.

The Charles H. Wright Museum of African-American History has more than 20,000 artifacts and archival materials.

Felicia Taylor Photo

◆ Mexicantown, near the Ambassador Bridge, is a Mexican-American business district divided by I-75. From cantinas featuring perfect margaritas to tortilla factories, the neighborhood has a wealth of Hispanic culture. The Mexicantown Mercado is an annual fiesta held every Sunday beginning in late June and lasting all summer. Cinco de Mayo parade on, naturally, the Fifth of May.

◆ Stuffed dumplings called pierogis are the main course in Hamtramck, a city within a city just two miles square that has been a Polish enclave since the first World War. Polish bakeries, meat shops, gift shops, bookstores and clubs line Joseph Campau Avenue. The city is also home to painters, potters, sculptors and a lively nightclub scene. Hamtramck (pronounced *Ham-Tram-Ick*) has a Strawberry Festival the first weekend in May at St. Florian Church and Mardi Gras (Fat Tuesday), where you can gorge yourself on fruit-filled paczki the day before the start of Lent.

◆ Dearborn, nine miles west of Detroit, is the center of the Middle Eastern community. Dozens of Arab restaurants, bakeries, groceries, meat markets, fruit markets and gift shops are located here. People come from all over to sample the fresh fruit drinks, pita bread and humous. The Arab-American Community Center for Economic and Social Service (ACCESS) features artifacts, photos, embroidered garments, calligraphy and other displays and an Arab International Festival is held on Warren Avenue each year in June or July. Ford Motor Company's world headquarters is located here.

Other Attractions

◆ The Detroit Zoo opened in 1928 and was the first in the nation to display animals in open exhibits without bars. The "Chimps of Harambee" exhibit, for example, is a 2.5-acre display where gorillas roam in a natural-like habitat surrounded by a moat. In another exhibit, birds fly freely in an indoor aviary. The zoo, located in Royal Oak, Michigan, has more than 1,000 animals representing more than 300 species in both indoor and outdoor exhibits. Its newest exhibit explores the exotic and delicate world of amphibians.

◆ Canbrook, located in Bloomfield Hills, is an internationally known center for art, education and science. The Cranbrook

Tigers are among the exotic animals in the Detroit Zoo collection.

Vito Palmisano, MDCVB

Institute of Science is a natural history museum featuring a large mineral collection, planetarium, physics hall and a 15-foot tyrannosaurus rex. It opened in 1999 as part of a multi-million dollar renovation and expansion at Cranbrook.

◆ The Detroit Historical Museum on Woodward tells the history of southeast Michigan through displays such as "Streets of Old Detroit," which recreates street scenes from 1840s, 1870s and 1990s Detroit, and "Motor City," which traces the history of automaking. The museum also operates the Dossin Great Lakes Museum on Belle Isle and Historic Fort Wayne, southwest of the city, a star-shaped fort built in the 1840s, which is open only during special events or by appointment.

Metropolitan Detroit Convention & Visitors Bureau

The city stores its treasures from the past at the Detroit Historical Museum.

◆ The Detroit Institute of Arts on Woodward is considered among the top five fine arts museums in the country. Its 100 galleries contain works of art from prehistory through the 20th century.

◆ Holocaust Memorial Center in West Bloomfield is the nation's first memorial dedicated exclusively to this tragic event in world history. Exhibits include Nazi propaganda, photographs, yellow stars and authentic identification papers. Admission is free.

Shopping

Metropolitan Detroit has about 150 large shopping centers including 23 major malls.

◆ Somerset Collection, located off I-75 in Troy, is an upscale mall — actually two malls connected by a 700-foot skywalk across Big Beaver Road. With stores such as Neiman Marcus, Tiffany & Co., Saks Fifth Avenue and Nordstrom, the shopping center rivals Chicago's Miracle Mile or New York's Madison Avenue.

◆ Great Lakes Crossing in Auburn Hills, about an hour north of Detroit, is the newest shopping mall and has more than 200 stores including a Bass Pro Outdoor World store the size of five football fields.

◆ Fairlane Town Centre in Dearborn is a major regional mall with more than 220 stores on three levels.

Somerset Collection in Troy is an upscale mall, actually two malls connected by a 700-foot skywalk.

Mike Ditz, MDCVB

Special Events

♦ Each Thanksgiving, 85 million people around the United States begin their holiday by watching America's Thanksgiving Parade, broadcast live from downtown Detroit. The parade is a tradition begun more than 70 years ago. More than a million people line the two-mile parade route on Woodward Avenue to wait for Santa Claus to arrive in the grand finale.

♦ The International Freedom Festival, celebrated in Detroit and Windsor, is a two-week celebration of international friendship starting in late June and spanning Canada Day (July 1) and the Fourth of July. Three million people annually attend the festival, which includes more than 50 free events and culminates with the largest fireworks display in the world. Hudson's department store, which is based in Detroit, has sponsored the festival since it began in 1959.

♦ On the third full weekend in September, 15 blocks of the University Cultural Center are filled with music, food and the works of more than 100 artists for the Detroit Festival of the Arts.

♦ The Michigan State Fair, a tradition since 1849, is the oldest state fair in the nation. It is held in late August at Michigan State Exposition Center at Eight Mile Road and Woodward Avenue in the city.

The Hudson's Freedom Festival is known for the largest fireworks display anywhere.

Vito Palmisano, MDCVB

More Information

Automotive Hall of Fame
21400 Oakwood Boulevard
Dearborn, MI 48121
313-240-4000
www.automotivehalloffame.com

Detroit Zoological Institute
(Detroit Zoo, Belle Isle Zoo, Belle Isle Aquarium)
8450 W. Ten Mile Road
Royal Oak, MI 48068
www.detroitzoo.org

Henry Ford Museum & Greenfield Village
20900 Oakwood Blvd.
Dearborn, MI 48124-4088
313-271-1620
24 Hour Recorded Information: (313) 982-6150
www.hfmgv.org

Metropolitan Detroit Convention and Visitors Bureau
211 West Fort Street
Detroit, MI 48226
800-DETROIT
www.visitdetroit.com

Motown Historical Museum
2648 W. Grand Boulevard
Detroit, MI 48208

Index

Michigan Index

New York Index

Ohio Index

Ontario Index

Pennsylvania Index

Lake Erie Books

For an extensive list of links to websites about Lake Erie, including those listed in this book, go to: www.LakeErieBooks.com

A Superb Walleye Fishing Guide to Lake Erie!

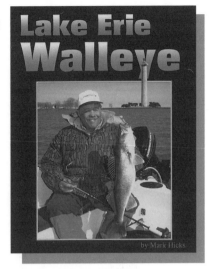

8 1/2" x 11" ~ paperback ~ 128 pages
106 photos ~ 32 illustrations ~ 7 maps
ISBN 0-9643309-1-1

LAKE ERIE WALLEYE will help anyone catch more and bigger walleyes from Lake Erie, the undisputed *Walleye Capital of the World*. Top guides and professional anglers tell where and how to take trophy walleyes from Lake Erie's clearer water.

"This has to be one of the most complete and best-presented fishing guidebooks devoted to a single Great Lake."
Dennis Knickerbocker, *Lansing State Journal,*
Lansing, Michigan.

ORDER NOW!

ONLY $14.95
plus $3.00 shipping & handling.
(Ohio Residents add $0.93 tax.)

Send Checks To:
BIG RIVER PRESS
P.O. Box 130
Millfield, OH 45761

CREDIT Card Orders Call:1-800-447-8238

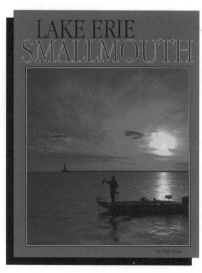

The Smallmouth Bass Fishing Guide to Lake Erie!

INCLUDES 41 FISH LOCATION MAPS!

148 BIG 8 1/2" x 11" pages ~ paperback
69 photos ~ 27 illustrations ~ 41 maps
ISBN 0-9643309-3-8

"There is so much information in 'Lake Erie Smallmouth' it's impossible to cover it all in a single column. But take my word for it, this is an informative and quality book designed for smallmouth bass fishing buffs who want to learn all the best techniques for catching these pugnacious fish."
Don Lewis, *Leader Times,* **Kittanning, PA.**

ORDER NOW!

ONLY $14.95
plus $3.50 shipping & handling.
(Ohio Residents add $0.93 tax.)

Send Checks To:
BIG RIVER PRESS
P.O. Box 130
Millfield, OH 45761

CREDIT Card Orders Call:1-800-447-8238